COOKING
NATURALLY
Recipes for good health

Pamela Westland

Vegetables

If wholefoods and healthy foods were chosen on appearance alone, fresh vegetables would have few rivals: perhaps only fresh fruits would pip them at the post for sheer appetite appeal.

Cash in on this great plus factor and serve vegetables fresh whenever possible. Not only because they have such eye appeal, but because this is when they are at their most nutritious.

All vegetables are high in vitamins, either singly or in various combinations, and contain significant amounts of minerals, mainly calcium and potassium. Carrots – in common with other orange and red vegetables such as pumpkin, red peppers and tomatoes – are a strong source of vitamin A (carotene). Broccoli and spinach have vitamins A, B1 (thiamine), B2 (riboflavin) and C in abundance, and both cauliflower and potatoes are high in vitamins B1 and C. Mushrooms, green peas, spinach and watercress are good sources of iron.

Sadly, vitamins are soluble in water and dissipate even on exposure to heat, light and air. So for this reason it is best – without actually going to the lengths of munching on raw potato sticks – to serve vegetables raw in salads and as crudités with dips, pastes and dressings.

Even though as much as 40 per cent of vitamins B1 and B2 and up to 60 per cent of vitamin C may be lost in the cooking process, you cannot expect to consign family and friends to a diet of raw Brussels sprouts and garden peas (though I do have a friend whose favourite June breakfast is a plate of fat peapods and strawberries!). What is important is to prepare, cook and serve vegetables with as little time-lag as possible: as near as you can get to serving them ''straight from the garden''. In practical terms this means, at best, growing your own, or shopping about every other day from the local farmers' market or foodstore which has the fastest turnover.

Cook vegetables for the shortest time you can get away with – it's probably best to wean the family away from very tender vegetables in gradual stages, otherwise they might be tempted to send them back to the kitchen! Use the minimum amount of water when boiling – or rather simmering – vegetables, for fast-boiling releases even more vitamins. Steaming them over lightly salted water or, better still, stock, is preferable.

Never peel vegetables unless you really have to, perhaps if the skins are damaged or discolored – as so many of the nutrients are just beneath the skin. Potato skins illustrate how good they can be; small whole potatoes simmered or steamed in their skins are almost as good. Scrubbing all root vegetables with a stiff brush is a lot easier and quicker than peeling: so the method has time and motion study on its side, too!

Dried beans and peas

These are a very special type of vegetable, the dried seeds of leguminous plants, which is to say, all peas and beans. In this dried state they can be safely stored in an airtight container for at least a year – a great advantage in former times – though the longer the interval since harvest the longer they will take to cook. For this reason, cooking times in recipes can only be approximate.

All beans have a high nutritional value, containing vitamins of the B group, proteins and calcium, iron and potassium in significant amounts. If they are combined in the same course with any grain or dairy product, then together they will provide all the amino acids the body needs – just as first-class proteins such as meat and fish do.

With the exception of lentils, all dried beans need to be pre-soaked, to rehydrate them, before cooking, either in cold water overnight or, once they have been brought to the boil from cold, for 1 hour. Never add salt until the beans are almost cooked – it is almost impossible to soften them – but cook them with all the flavoring vegetables (herbs, onions, garlic, celery and carrots) and spices you like.

The word of warning on page 63 bears repetition: **always fast-boil kidney beans for (to be safe) 15-20 minutes to get rid of harmful toxins.** Then and only then may they be added to stews, casseroles and soups.

Beans and peas come in all shapes and sizes, from the large milky white lima beans, so good with boiled bacon, to the small pink speckled pinto or Mexican beans; tiny bright green mung beans – the fertile seed of Chinese bean sprouts – and jet black kidney beans, the heart of African soul food; the elegant pale green flageolets, superb with garlicky lamb, and deep red kidney beans, the vehicle for red-hot chili seasoning. Their uses – in soups, salads, dips, stews, casseroles, quiches and pies – is just as versatile.

Grains

Named after the Roman goddess of the harvest, Ceres, cereals or grains are the edible seeds of plants bred from wild grasses. They include wheat – especially important because it is the only one to produce flour with good rising properties – rice, corn, barley, oats, rye, millet and buckwheat.

In their natural state, stripped only of the inedible outer husk, grains are highly nutritious. In the refined or processed form, as white flour, white rice and pearl barley, they have been stripped of the germ, which contains vitamins of the B group, vitamin E, calcium, potassium, iron, copper, magnesium and fat, and the bran, packed with dietary fibre.

On the subject of terms, the very words used to describe the various types of flour and bread set a trap for the unwary. Whole wheat, whole meal and whole grain are synonymous, and mean just what they say. The flour has been milled from the whole grain, and includes the germ and the bran. Sometimes a percentage of the germ and bran have been removed; if so, exactly what percentage is often indicated in an accompanying figure. For example, 81 per cent and 85 per cent whole meal flour have had 19 per cent and 15 per cent respectively extracted. Since the term whole meal is so vague it can be – and is – applied to "brown" flour. And this, like "brown" sugar, can be nothing more than the refined (incomplete) white product, colored.

By switching to whole wheat flour for all baking – not only bread, but pastry, biscuits and cakes – to whole wheat pasta made with the whole durum (hard) wheat flour and to brown rice, you are well on the way to a healthy and wholefood diet. Brown rice does take longer to cook than white (45 minutes as against 10-12 minutes) so when time is of the essence, opt for pasta. Whole wheat pasta, so superb with simple and quick vegetable sauces, is cooked to perfection in 10-12 minutes.

Each grain brings its own characteristic flavor to a dish, and recipes follow to fire your imagination to turn those staple foods into satisfying and homely fare – a casserole of vegetable and oats, a chicken and mushroom risotto using wheat groats instead of rice, croquettes of vegetables with cracked wheat (bulgar) all prove the point deliciously.

Don't neglect these other whole grains when it comes to accompaniments for meat and vegetables. Soak them overnight if possible in cold water, rinse and drain them and cook them in boiling water for 1-1½ hours. Or if time presses, buy the cracked grains which can be cooked in 15 minutes or so.

Dairy products

"A little of what you fancy does you good" must surely be true of all those deliciously wholesome foods from the dairy. For whole milk, whole milk products, butter, cheese and eggs are good sources of vitamins A and D (much of the vitamin C is destroyed in pasteurizing), vitamins B1 (thiamine) and B2 (riboflavin), proteins and minerals – calcium, potassium and phosphorus. That's on the plus side.

What makes so many people now switch to low-fat skimmed milk, polyunsaturated vegetable margarine, low-fat yogurt and cottage cheese is the high fat and cholesterol content of whole milk.

Yogurt, which has become such a popular instant snack or dessert, has many uses in the kitchen. You will find it gives a delicious sharpness to cheese sauces – on baked vegetables, for example – makes a dreamy topping for everything from desserts to soup and salads, and can be used in place of cream in mousses and ices.

Yogurt tends to separate unattractively when it is heated in liquid sauces, as when it is stirred into a casserole. Prevent this by stabilizing the yogurt (see page 12).

Fats and oils

Medical experts have at last drummed into us that a high saturated fat intake is a major factor in the incidence of heart disease, the greatest single cause of death in the Western world. And a recent report by the British National Advisory Committee on Nutrition Education has made practical recommendations on how painlessly, so to speak, every family can reduce the amount of fat it consumes each day. There are three groups.

Saturated fats, the ones which set solid at

room temperature, are mainly of animal origin (though coconuts have them in abundance too) and are the worst offenders. They are present in all whole dairy products – milk, whole-milk yogurt, butter, cream and cheese – and in meat and meat products, not only in the obvious fat around a piece of steak or a lamb chop or the lumps of fat in salami, but the "hidden" fat that marbles all red meats.

Polyunsaturated fats are liquid or soft at room temperature and are present as oil in fish, to a smaller extent in meats, and in plants. These plant oils are extracted for a number of domestic and industrial uses, most familiar perhaps as cooking and salad oils. Corn, sunflower, safflower and soy bean oils are high in polyunsaturates. It is this category of oils that is said to have the ability actually to lower the level of cholesterol – a fatty, wax-like substance – in the bloodstream.

The last category, the mono-unsaturated fats, seem to have little or no effect on the incidence of heart disease; to be neutral in effect. Olive oil is high in this type of fatty acids.

When it comes to assessing fat types and levels, margarines can cause a great deal of confusion. Some, the hard types sold in blocks, are made up of saturated (solid) fats; some soft margarines, sold in cartons, are high in polyunsaturates and some, known as "low-fat", are actually a blend of hard margarines and water. Until you are familiar with the various properties of each brand, it pays to check the label.

At present far too much of our body energy (or calorie intake) is derived from fats – 38 per cent. The NACNE Report recommends that this should be cut to 34 per cent in five years' time and 30 per cent over a ten-year period, with the axe falling most heavily on saturated fats. As the Report also recommends an increase (to compensate) in carbohydrates, and in dietary fibre, in practical terms this means less red meats, less wholemilk dairy produce and more bread and cereals. A chicken instead of a joint of beef on Sunday, and a cottage cheese and date sandwich instead of a ham one.

Fruit and dried fruit

Fruits must surely be the most delicious convenience food of all, and of course they are absolutely brimful of nourishment. All fruits are high in vitamin C, with blackcurrants at the top of the class. The yellow-colored fruits especially – that's melons, apricots, peaches and gooseberries – are a good source of vitamin A (carotene) and dried fruits weigh heavily with thiamine (vitamin B1).

As it is with vegetables, so it is with fruits: cooking can destroy up to 50 per cent of the vitamin C and even "open" freezing (without syrup) destroys about 20 per cent. So fresh fruit on the menu – for breakfast, lunch or supper – at least once a day makes sound nutritional sense.

Dried fruits are in effect the very essence of fresh fruits, being much more concentrated purveyors of the natural sugars, fructose, glucose and sucrose, and of dietary fibre. Fresh apricots, for example, consist of about 2 per cent fibre, dried apricots ten times as much.

Get into the habit of chopping up dried fruits to add to muesli; tossing a handful of dried vine fruits – raisins, sultanas and currants – into rice just before serving, and into salads and fruit salads; and using dried fruits increasingly to cut down on sugars and you will have captured the spirit of wholefood cookery.

Salt

The way some people punish the salt shaker you'd think their lives depended on it. And they could well do. Recent researches have shown an excess intake of salt to be responsible for hypertension (and 40 per cent of us are prey to that), heart disease and brain haemorrhage.

Apparently we need only 500 milligrams a day of salt; or, more specifically, we need the 200 milligrams of sodium that it contains. But in general we have been treating our taste buds to very much more. Not all of this salt is shaken on to our plates at the table, of course. Processed foods of all kinds are laden with it.

You will find it easier to cut down on salt in cooking vegetables, rice, sauces and so on if you add herbs and spices. Fresh mint, marjoram or parsley with the vegetables, a touch of cinnamon or allspice with whole grains, a couple of bay leaves in the sauce, and who needs salt!

By preparing and serving fresh ingredients, in wholefood cooking we have the greatest possible measure of control over what we eat. And we can be confident that the food we serve is as natural, wholesome and delicious as can be. I hope the following recipes prove the point.

SOUPS, STARTERS & SNACKS

There's a very fine line drawn these days between snacks, light lunch or supper dishes, starters and appetizers to serve with drinks. In this chapter we bring together ideas to suit all those occasions.

Fruit is high on the wholefood list of light and lovely ways to start a meal; the fish, egg and cheese dishes make substantial snacks to serve with whole wheat toast, crisp, crunchy sticks of fresh vegetables or a light salad; and whether they are warm and welcoming for the winter or chilled and refreshing for summer, soups are a versatile example of wholefood cooking.

A good stock gives them "body" and brings out the full flavor of the other ingredients. You get the best results by making your own, using beef bones (roasted first on a tray in a moderate oven for 40-45 minutes), or a cooked or uncooked chicken carcass with chopped onions, carrots, celery and a bunch of herbs for flavoring. Cover with water, bring slowly to the boil, cover and simmer for 2-2½ hours. Strain, cool and store in the refrigerator or freezer. For a vegetable stock use well-washed vegetable peelings and trimmings with some herbs to intensify the flavor.

ALMOND SOUP

Serves 4

4½ cups chicken stock
2 celery stalks, chopped
1 small onion, peeled and quartered
1 bouquet garni
2 bay leaves
1 mace blade
salt
freshly ground white pepper
1½ cups blanched almonds, ground
½ cup sweet sherry
½ cup plain unsweetened yogurt
(see note below)
2 tablespoons flaked almonds, toasted,
to garnish

Preparation time: 15 minutes
Cooking time: 1 hour

If you use homemade yogurt, it will need to be stabilized before adding to the soup, otherwise it might separate. To do this, stir in 1 teaspoon flour and heat gently in a small pan, stirring constantly.

1. Put the stock into a pan, add the celery, onion, bouquet garni, bay leaves and mace and season with salt and pepper.
2. Bring slowly to the boil, uncovered, and skim off any foam from the top. Cover the pan and simmer for about 25 minutes.
3. Strain the stock, discarding the flavorings, and return it to the pan.
4. Stir in the ground almonds, add the sherry, cover and simmer for 20 minutes. **F**
5. Stir in the yogurt and heat gently. Taste and adjust seasoning if necessary.
6. Scatter the soup with the toasted almonds. Serve hot.

F *Freeze for up to 3 months. Thaw at room temperature for 4-5 hours, then reheat and continue from step 5.*

CHINESE BEAN-SPROUT SOUP

Serves 4

4½ cups chicken stock
1 medium onion, peeled and quartered
2 carrots, scraped and quartered
4 scallions, thinly sliced
225 g (8 oz) fresh bean-sprouts
salt
freshly ground black pepper
2 tablespoons soy sauce
2 tablespoons dry sherry
2 large radishes, sliced and quartered, to garnish

GINGERED PUMPKIN SOUP

Serves 6

2¼ lb slice of pumpkin, peeled, pitted and roughly
chopped
1 piece fresh ginger root, peeled
1 tablespoon sunflower oil
1 large onion, peeled and chopped
2 teaspoons ground ginger
1 teaspoon ground turmeric
2 large, ripe tomatoes, skinned and chopped
2 teaspoons soft light brown sugar
¼ teaspoon grated nutmeg
strip thinly-pared orange rind
2½ cups chicken stock
salt
freshly ground black pepper
1¼ cups plain unsweetened yogurt
(stabilized if homemade, see page 12)
To garnish:
2 tablespoons chopped parsley
6 tablespoons pumpkin seeds

Preparation time: 15 minutes
Cooking time: 40 minutes

1. Put the pumpkin into a pan with the piece of ginger and cover it with water. Bring to the boil, cover the pan and simmer for 15 minutes, or until the pumpkin is tender. Drain thoroughly and remove the ginger.
2. Heat the oil in the pan and fry the onion over moderate heat for 2 minutes. Stir in the ground ginger and turmeric and cook for 1 minute.
3. Add the pumpkin, tomatoes, sugar, nutmeg, orange rind and stock and bring to the boil. Cover and simmer for 10 minutes. Cool slightly. Discard the orange rind. F
4. Liquidize the pumpkin mixture in a blender, then return the purée to the pan. Season with salt and pepper and stir in the yogurt. Heat gently. Taste and adjust seasoning if necessary.
5. Garnish the soup with the parsley and pumpkin seeds.

F *Freeze for up to 3 months. Thaw at room temperature for 4-5 hours, then reheat and continue from step 4.*

Preparation time: 15 minutes
Cooking time: 30 minutes

1. Put the stock in a pan with the onion and carrots, bring to the boil, cover and simmer for 20 minutes.
2. Strain the stock thoroughly and discard all the vegetables.
3. Return the stock to the pan, add the thinly sliced scallions and bean-sprouts, and season with salt and pepper. Bring to the boil and simmer gently for 2-3 minutes.
4. Stir in the soy sauce and sherry, taste and adjust seasoning if necessary.
5. Serve the soup in individual dishes and garnish each one with radish slices.

From the left: Almond soup; Chinese bean-sprout soup; Gingered pumpkin soup.

CELERY ROOT AND ORANGE SOUP

Serves 6

1 large celery root, about 12 oz, peeled and roughly chopped
1 medium potato, peeled and roughly chopped
2 medium carrots, scraped and sliced
4½ cups chicken stock
thinly pared rind of ½ orange
1 teaspoon grated orange rind
1 tablespoon orange juice
salt
freshly ground black pepper
6 tablespoons plain unsweetened yogurt
(stabilized if homemade, see page 12)

Preparation time: 20 minutes
Cooking time: 45 minutes

1. Put the celery root, potato and carrots into a pan with the stock and bring to the boil. Cover the pan and simmer for 30 minutes, or until all the vegetables are soft.

2. Cut the orange rind into very thin matchstick strips. Place them in a saucepan with a little boiling water and boil for 10 minutes, then drain. Reserve for garnish.

3. Cool the vegetables and stock slightly, then liquidize in a blender.

4. Return the purée to the pan, add the grated orange rind and juice and season with salt and pepper. Bring back to the boil and simmer for 5 minutes. ⅎ

5. To serve, pour the soup into individual dishes or bowls, swirl 1 tablespoon yogurt on to each portion and garnish with strips of orange rind.

ⅎ *Freeze for up to 3 months. Thaw at room temperature for 4-5 hours, then reheat and continue from step 5.*

CURRIED CAULIFLOWER SOUP

Serves 4

1 tablespoon sunflower oil
1 medium onion, peeled and sliced
2 teaspoons curry powder (or to taste)
1 small cauliflower, roughly chopped
3¾ cups chicken stock
salt
freshly ground black pepper
4 tablespoons sunflower seeds, to garnish

Preparation time: 15 minutes
Cooking time: 30 minutes

1. Heat the oil in a large pan and fry the onion over moderate heat for 2 minutes. Stir in the curry powder and cook for 1 minute.

2. Add the cauliflower and stock, season with salt and pepper and bring to the boil. Cover the pan and simmer for 20 minutes.

3. Cool slightly, then liquidize the vegetables and stock in a blender. F

4. Return the purée to the pan. Taste and adjust the seasoning if necessary and reheat.

5. Garnish the soup with the sunflower seeds.

Variation: *To add interesting texture to the soup, cut off a few very small cauliflower florets before blending and set them aside. Add them to the purée in the pan.*

F *Freeze for up to 3 months. Thaw at room temperature for 4-5 hours, then reheat and garnish with sunflower seeds.*

CORN SOUP

Serves 6-8

6¼ cups chicken stock
1 medium onion, thinly sliced
1 medium leek, white part only, thinly sliced
2 medium potatoes, peeled and diced
salt
freshly ground black pepper
⅔ cup milk or buttermilk
12 oz corn cobs
6 oz can baby corn (from Oriental food stores),
(optional)
2 tablespoons chopped parsley

Preparation time: 15 minutes
Cooking time: 30 minutes

1. Put the stock into a large pan with the onion, leek and potatoes, season with salt and pepper and bring to the boil. Cover the pan and simmer for 20 minutes. Cool slightly, then liquidize in a blender. F

2. Return the puree to the pan and stir in the milk. Add the corn and baby corn, if using, and heat gently.

3. Taste and adjust the seasoning. Stir in the parsley. Serve hot.

F *Freeze for up to 3 months. Thaw at room temperature for 3-4 hours, then continue from step 2.*

From the left: Celery root and orange soup; Curried cauliflower soup; corn soup.

1. Heat the oil in a large pan. Fry the onion and garlic over a moderate heat for 4-5 minutes, stirring once or twice. Add the carrots, celery and potato, pour on the stock and add the tomatoes. Add the bouquet garni and season with salt and pepper.
2. Bring to the boil, cover the pan and simmer for 30 minutes, stirring occasionally. ℱ
3. Add the macaroni, beans and zucchini, return to the boil, cover and cook for a further 15 minutes.
4. Taste and adjust the seasoning if necessary. Discard the bouquet garni and stir in the parsley. Serve hot, with the cheese handed separately.

ℱ *Freeze for up to 3 months. Thaw at room temperature for 4-5 hours, then reheat over a low heat and continue from Step 3.*

WATERCRESS SOUP

Serves 6

2 tablespoons butter
1 medium onion, peeled and finely chopped
3 scallions, sliced
3 bunches watercress, trimmed and chopped
¼ cup whole wheat flour
4½ cups chicken stock
salt
freshly ground black pepper
⅔ cup plain unsweetened yogurt (stabilized if homemade, see page 12)
small sprigs of watercress, to garnish

Preparation time: 15 minutes
Cooking time: 40 minutes

1. Melt the butter in a large pan and fry the onion, scallions and watercress over a low heat for 10 minutes, stirring frequently.
2. Increase the heat to moderate, and gradually pour on the stock, stirring constantly. Season with salt and pepper, bring to the boil and cover the pan.
3. Simmer for 15 minutes.
4. Cool slightly, then liquidize in a blender. ℱ
5. Return the purée to the pan, stir in the yogurt, taste and adjust seasoning if necessary. Reheat gently.
6. Serve the soup hot, garnished with the watercress sprigs.

ℱ *Freeze for up to 3 months. Thaw at room temperature for 3-4 hours, then continue from step 5.*

PASTA MINESTRONE

Serves 6-8

1 tablespoon sunflower oil
1 large onion, peeled and chopped
1 garlic clove, peeled and chopped
2 medium carrots, scraped and thinly sliced
2 tender celery stalks, thinly sliced
1 large potato, peeled and diced
6¼ cups beef stock
12 oz tomatoes, peeled and sliced
1 bouquet garni
salt
freshly ground black pepper
4 oz whole wheat short-cut macaroni
1 cup dried beans, boiled until tender and drained
2 zucchini, cut into matchstick strips
3½ tablespoons chopped parsley
grated Parmesan cheese, to serve

Preparation time: 15 minutes
Cooking time: 1 hour

RED PEPPER SOUP

Serves 4-6

1 tablespoon sunflower oil
1 large onion, peeled and chopped
2 garlic cloves, peeled and finely chopped
2 tablespoons sherry
3 large red peppers, seeded, cored and cut into
strips
1 medium potato, peeled and diced
2½ tablespoons tomato paste
2 large tomatoes, peeled and sliced
4½ cups beef stock
1 bay leaf
1 bouquet garni
salt
freshly ground black pepper
To garnish:
2 tablespoons plain unsweetened yogurt
sprigs of parsley or chervil

Preparation time: 15 minutes
Cooking time: 45 minutes

1. Heat the oil in a large pan and fry the onion over moderate heat for 4-5 minutes, stirring once or twice. Add the garlic and the sherry and stir well.
2. Stir in the peppers, potato, tomato paste and tomatoes and pour on the hot stock. Add the bay leaf and bouquet garni and season with salt and pepper. Stir well.
3. Bring to the boil, cover the pan and simmer for 30 minutes.
4. With a slotted spoon, remove 2 spoonfuls of peppers and set aside.
5. Discard the bay leaf and bouquet garni and liquidize the soup in a blender. **F**
6. Return the soup to the pan, stir in the peppers, taste and adjust seasoning and heat gently.
7. Garnish the soup with swirls of yogurt and sprigs of chervil or parsley. Serve hot.

F *Freeze for up to 3 months. Thaw at room temperature for 4-5 hours, then continue from Step 6.*

Left, from the top: Pasta minestrone; Watercress soup. Below: Red pepper soup.

APRICOT SESAME SOUP

Serves 6

1½ cups dried apricots, soaked overnight
2 medium carrots, scraped and sliced
1 medium onion, peeled and sliced
1 cinnamon stick
2 cups chicken stock
2½ teaspoons lemon juice
salt
freshly ground black pepper
⅔ cup plain unsweetened yogurt
1 tablespoon light honey (optional)
2 tablespoons sesame seeds, to garnish

Preparation time: 15 minutes, plus overnight soaking
Cooking time: 1 hour 10 minutes

1. Drain the apricots and measure 2½ cups of the soaking water. Make the liquid up to that measure if necessary.
2. Put the apricots, liquid, carrots, onion, cinnamon, stock and lemon juice into a large pan and season with salt and pepper.
3. Bring to the boil, cover the pan and simmer for 1 hour. Remove the cinnamon stick. Skim off any fat that has risen to the surface. Allow the soup to cool, then liquidize in a blender. **F**
4. Beat in the yogurt. Taste and adjust seasoning if necessary. Chill the soup and serve it with a little honey drizzled over and garnished with the sesame seeds, in chilled bowls.

Variation: *You can also serve the soup hot, accompanied by oyster crackers. Stir in the yogurt after blending the soup, then reheat it gently.*

F *Freeze for up to 3 months. Thaw at room temperature for 4-5 hours, then continue from step 4.*

From the left: Apricot sesame soup; Gazpacho; Mushroom dairy soup.

To garnish:
½ cucumber, finely diced
1 red pepper, seeded, cored and finely chopped
1 green pepper, seeded, cored and finely chopped
4 scallions, thinly sliced
2½ tablespoons finely snipped chives
8 Spanish olives, thinly sliced
2 tablespoons chopped parsley

Preparation time: 30 minutes, plus 1 hour chilling

1. Liquidize all the main ingredients in batches in a blender. Taste and adjust the seasoning if necessary.
2. Cover the soup and chill in the refrigerator for at least 1 hour.
3. Stir all the garnish ingredients into the soup. Serve chilled, in chilled bowls.

MUSHROOM DAIRY SOUP

Serves 4

1 lb small mushrooms
2½ cups chicken stock, all fat removed
1 medium onion, peeled and sliced
½-1 teaspoon ground coriander
salt
freshly ground black pepper
2½ cups buttermilk
2 tablespoons chopped mint

Preparation time: 15 minutes, plus chilling
Cooking time: 15 minutes

1. Reserve a few of the best-shaped mushrooms for garnish. Chop the remainder.
2. Put the mushrooms in a pan with the stock, onion and coriander and season with salt and pepper. Bring to the boil and skim off any fat that rises to the surface. Cover and simmer for 10 minutes. Cool slightly.
3. Liquidize the vegetables and stock in a blender. Cool. **F**
4. Beat in the buttermilk. Cover and chill.
5. Just before serving, stir in the mint. Thinly slice the reserved mushrooms and scatter them over the soup to garnish.

GAZPACHO

Serves 6-8

1 lb tomatoes, peeled and sliced
3¾ cups chicken stock, all fat removed
½ cucumber, peeled and chopped
1 garlic clove, peeled and chopped
1 green pepper, seeded, cored and sliced
1 cup diced whole wheat bread, crusts removed
4 tablespoons sunflower oil
salt
freshly ground black pepper
2 tablespoons red wine vinegar

F *Freeze for up to 3 months. Thaw at room temperature for 3-4 hours, then continue from step 4.*

VEGETABLE VELVET

Serves 6

1 large eggplant, about 8 oz
6 tablespoons cream cheese with herbs
½ cup curd cheese
1 tablespoon lemon juice
1 tablespoon chopped chervil or parsley
salt
freshly ground black pepper
1 lemon, quartered, to serve

Preparation time: 20 minutes
Cooking time: 45 minutes
Oven: 375°F

A blend of eggplant and creamy cheeses, this dish makes a delicious dip to serve as an appetizer or with drinks. It is also a good sandwich filling, especially with rye whole wheat bread. It is best made no more than a few hours in advance. Store in the refrigerator in a lidded container.

1. Prick the skin of the eggplant with a fork and place it on a cookie sheet.
2. Cook the eggplant in a preheated oven for 45 minutes, turning it once or twice.
3. Cut the eggplant in half lengthways and scoop out the flesh.
4. Purée the eggplant flesh in a blender with the cheeses and lemon juice. Stir in the herb and season with salt and pepper.
5. Pile the mixture into a serving bowl and garnish with the lemon wedges. If liked surround the dish with fresh vegetable sticks – crudités, see page 26 – on slices of warm whole wheat pitta bread.

BAKED AVOCADOS

Serves 4

2 avocados, halved and seeded
2½ teaspoons lemon juice
1 cup plain unsweetened yogurt
2 tablespoons tomato paste
8 oz fresh or thawed frozen crab meat, flaked
2½ tablespoons grated Parmesan cheese
1 shallot, peeled and finely chopped
salt
freshly ground black pepper
large pinch of cayenne pepper
2 eggs, beaten

From the left: Vegetable velvet; Baked avocados.
Opposite: Melon kontiki.

Preparation time: 15 minutes
Cooking time: 30 minutes
Oven: 350°F

1. Crunch up 4 pieces of foil in a baking dish and stand the halved avocados on them, making sure they are level. Brush the cut surfaces with lemon juice.
2. Beat together the plain unsweetened yogurt and tomato paste. Stir in the crab meat, cheese, shallot and the remaining lemon juice and season with salt and pepper and cayenne. Beat in the eggs.
3. Divide the filling between the avocado halves.
4. Pour water into the dish to come halfway up the avocado shells. Cook in a preheated oven for 25-30 minutes, until the filling is set. Serve at once.

MELON KONTIKI

Serves 4

1 large cantaloupe or honeydew melon, quartered and seeded
2 tablespoons port
1 tablespoon ginger syrup
2 kiwi fruits, peeled and sliced into rounds
matchstick strips of candied ginger, to decorate

Preparation time: 15 minutes, plus about 30 minutes chilling

1. With a long, sharp knife, cut the melon flesh away from the rind, but leave it in place.
2. Stir the port and ginger syrup together and pour over the melon slices. Cover and chill for at least 30 minutes.
3. Cut the melon flesh into ½ inch slices. Leaving each pointed-end slice intact, push alternate slices to left and right.
4. Arrange slices of kiwi fruit in a line down the center of each melon slice. Decorate with strips of ginger and serve chilled.

ELIZABETHAN EGGS

Serves 4

2 tablespoons butter
1 small onion, peeled and very finely chopped
1 lb young sorrel leaves, stripped from stems
1¼ tablespoons lemon juice
salt
freshly ground black pepper
6 hard-cooked eggs, shelled and halved

Preparation time: 15 minutes
Cooking time: 15 minutes

Sorrel, a leafy herb with a lemony scent, was very popular in England in Elizabethan times. If it is unavailable, you can use young and tender spinach leaves instead.

1. Melt the butter in a pan and fry the onion over low heat for 5 minutes, stirring occasionally.
2. Add the sorrel, mix well and add in the lemon juice. Season with salt and pepper. Simmer gently for 5 minutes, stirring frequently with a wooden spoon.
3. Chop 2 of the hard-cooked eggs, keeping the whites and yolks separate, and reserve.
4. Press the sorrel sauce through a sieve and gently reheat it.
5. Place the halved eggs, cut sides down, on a serving dish. Serve them with the sauce and garnish with pieces of the chopped egg. Serve at once, as an appetizer or a light meal, with whole wheat bread.

TANGY SWEET AND SOUR SALAD

Serves 6

1 small ruffled endive
2 small grapefruit (pink variety, if possible), peeled and segmented
2 small avocados, pitted, peeled and sliced
1 cup cottage cheese

TOMATO MOUSSE

Serves 4

2 tablespoons butter
1 small onion, chopped
1 garlic clove, finely chopped
6 large, ripe tomatoes, skinned, seeded and chopped
½ cup mushrooms, chopped
2 tablespoons mint leaves
½ teaspoon superfine sugar
salt
freshly ground black pepper
1 teaspoon lemon juice
few drops of Tabasco Sauce
2 tablespoons hot water
1 tablespoon powdered gelatin
⅔ cup sour cream
½ cucumber, to garnish

Preparation time: 20 minutes, plus setting
Cooking time: 20 minutes

1. Melt the butter in a pan and fry the onion and garlic over low heat for 5 minutes, stirring occasionally.
2. Add the tomatoes and mushrooms and continue cooking for 10 minutes, stirring frequently.
3. Remove from the heat and stir in the mint, sugar, salt, pepper, lemon juice and the Tabasco Sauce.
4. Put the hot water in a cup, sprinkle the gelatin on top and stir over hot water until it has dissolved. Stir the gelatin into the tomato mixture.
5. Liquidize the mixture in a blender. Taste the purée and adjust seasoning if necessary. Cool.
6. Stir the sour cream into the purée. Pour into a serving dish, cover and chill in the refrigerator for 2-3 hours to set. **F**
7. Using a potato peeler, pare off the cucumber peel in long, thin strips. Thinly slice the cucumber. Arrange the overlapping slices of cucumber around the dish.

F *Freeze the mousse for up to 1 month. Thaw overnight in the refrigerator.*

4 tablespoons golden raisins
1 teaspoon grapefruit rind, cut into julienne strips
2 oz toasted sesame seeds
Dressing:
2 tablespoons lemon juice
1 tablespoon light honey
6 tablespoons tomato juice
¼ teaspoon mustard powder
salt
freshly ground black pepper

Preparation time: 15 minutes

1. Arrange the largest endive leaves to cover a serving plate and make a 'nest' of the smallest ones in the center.
2. Combine the dressing ingredients and toss the grapefruit and avocado in the dressing.
3. Arrange a ring of alternating grapefruit and avocado slices around the plate on top of the endive. Pour over any remaining dressing.
4. Mix the cheese with the golden raisins and grapefruit rind, pile it in the center and scatter with sesame seeds.

From the left: Elizabethan eggs; Tangy sweet and sour salad; Tomato mousse.

GRILLED SHERRIED ORANGES

Serves 4

4 large oranges
4 tablespoons dry sherry
2 tablespoons orange liqueur
1 tablespoon light honey
To garnish:
3 tablespoons water
2 tablespoons light honey
16-20 white grapes, pitted

Preparation time: 15 minutes
Cooking time: 10 minutes

1. Halve the oranges. Cut out the segments and discard the pith. Reserve 4 half shells.
2. Heat the broiler to medium. In a small bowl mix together the sherry, liqueur, honey and the orange segments and pour into a small heat-proof dish.
3. Heat the water and honey for the garnish in a small pan over moderate heat and poach the grapes for 5 minutes.
4. Broil the oranges for 5 minutes, until they are hot. Pour them into the reserved orange shells.
5. Garnish the oranges with the grapes and serve at once.

GREEK-STYLE ONIONS

Serves 6

1 cup red wine
4 tablespoons red wine vinegar
3 tablespoons sunflower oil
3 tablespoons tomato paste
3 tablespoons light brown sugar
2 cups water
2¼ lb pearl onions, peeled
4 tender celery stalks, thinly sliced
4 oz seedless raisins
salt
freshly ground black pepper
3 tablespoons chopped parsley

Preparation time: 15 minutes
Cooking time: 45 minutes

1. Put the wine, vinegar, oil, tomato paste, sugar and water into a pan and stir over low heat to dissolve the sugar.
2. Add the onions, celery and raisins, season with salt and pepper and bring to the boil over moderate heat, stirring occasionally.
3. Cover the pan and simmer gently for 35 minutes, or until the onions are tender. Taste the sauce and adjust the seasoning if necessary.
4. Stir in 2 tablespoons of the parsley, and garnish with the remainder. Serve hot, with plenty of crusty whole wheat bread.

BAKED HERBY MUSHROOMS

Serves 4

16-20 medium mushrooms
2 tablespoons sunflower oil
1 small onion, peeled and finely chopped
2 garlic cloves, crushed
6 tablespoons fresh whole wheat breadcrumbs
¼ teaspoon grated nutmeg
3 tablespoons chopped parsley
8 tablespoons grated Gouda cheese
2 tablespoons plain unsweetened yogurt
1 egg, beaten
salt
freshly ground black pepper

Preparation time: 15 minutes
Cooking time: 20 minutes
Oven: 350°F

1. Cut the stalks from the mushrooms and trim and chop them finely.
2. Heat the oil in a skillet and fry the onion, garlic and chopped stalks over moderate heat for 3-4 minutes, stirring frequently.
3. Turn the mixture into a bowl and stir in the breadcrumbs, nutmeg, parsley, 4 tablespoons of the cheese and the yogurt. Bind the mixture with the beaten egg and season with salt and pepper.
4. Place the mushrooms, stalk side up, on a greased cookie sheet. Divide the filling between them. Sprinkle on the remaining cheese.
5. Bake in a preheated oven for 15 minutes, or until bubbling. Serve hot with triangles of toast.

Clockwise from top left: Greek-style onions; Baked herby mushrooms; Grilled sherried oranges.

CRUDITÉS WITH DIPS

Offer a selection of crisp, colorful vegetable 'dip-sticks' and savoury dips as appetizers to serve with drinks, or as a light and crunchy starter or snack.

Choose fresh, seasonal vegetables, and be sure you buy the best possible quality. Prepare them so that they are evenly matched for size – carrot, cucumber, celery and green pepper strips of equal length and thickness, trimmed scallions, sliced button mushrooms and cauliflower florets graded for size. You can prepare them a day in advance and store them, each type separately, in lidded containers in the refrigerator.

LIPTAUER CHEESE DIP

Serves 4-6

2 tablespoons butter
¾ cup curd cheese
1 teaspoon Dijon mustard
1 teaspoon anchovy paste
1 teaspoon paprika pepper, plus extra for garnish
1 tablespoon chopped gherkin
1 tablespoon chopped capers
1 teaspoon finely snipped chives, plus extra for garnish
freshly ground black pepper

Preparation time: 15 minutes

1. Beat the butter until it is soft. Beat in the cheese, mustard, anchovy and paprika and beat until the mixture is smooth. Stir in the gherkin, capers and chives and season with pepper.
2. Spoon the dip into a serving bowl and sprinkle on a little paprika and a few chopped chives to garnish.

CELERY DIP

Serves 4

¾ cup curd cheese
2 tablespoons plain unsweetened yogurt
3 tender celery stalks, finely chopped
2 tablespoons chopped celery leaves
1 teaspoon celery seeds
salt
freshly ground black pepper
chopped celery leaves, to garnish

Preparation time: 15 minutes

1. Beat the cheese and yogurt and stir in the chopped celery, leaves and seeds. Season with salt and pepper. **F**
2. Spoon the dip into a serving bowl and garnish with the celery leaves.

F *Freeze the dip for up to 2 months. Thaw at room temperature for 2 hours.*

From the left: Crudités; Liptauer cheese dip; Celery dip; Lima bean dip.

LIMA BEAN DIP

Serves 4

⅔ cup dry lima beans, soaked overnight
and drained
4 tablespoons sunflower oil
2 garlic cloves, crushed
2 tablespoons cider vinegar
2 tablespoons chopped parsley
salt
freshly ground black pepper
chopped parsley, to garnish

Preparation time: 15 minutes
Cooking time: 1 hour

1. Cook the beans in boiling unsalted water for 1 hour, or until they are tender. Drain them, reserving the liquid, rinse in cold water and drain again.
2. Liquidize the beans in a blender with the oil, garlic, vinegar and 3 tablespoons of the reserved liquid.
3. Stir in the parsley and season with salt and pepper. Garnish with the chopped parsley.

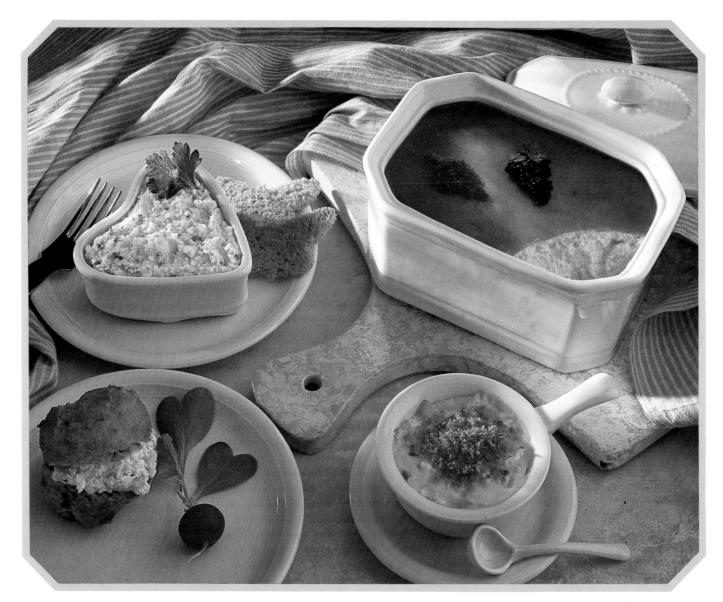

SHRIMP PUFFS

Serves 6

1¼ cups water
4 tablespoons margarine
1 cup whole wheat flour
1 teaspoon dried mixed herbs
pinch of salt
2 large eggs
Filling:
1 cup curd cheese
¾ cup shelled shrimp, chopped
1 tablespoon chopped parsley
1 teaspoon lemon juice
pinch of cayenne pepper
freshly ground black pepper

Preparation time: 30 minutes
Cooking time: 30 minutes
Oven: 400°F

1. In a small pan, heat the water and margarine to boiling point. Stir together the flour, herbs and salt. Tip the fat mixture at once on to the flour and stir vigorously. Beat in the eggs one at a time, beating continuously.
2. Using 2 dessertspoons to shape rounds of the mixture, place them well apart on a greased cookie sheet.
3. Bake in a preheated oven for 15-20 minutes, or until the buns are well risen and sound hollow when tapped.
4. Split the buns open to allow the steam to escape and leave them on a wire rack to cool. Store for up to 1 day in an airtight tin.
5. Beat the filling ingredients together. Fill the buns just before serving and accompany with a salad garnish.

Clockwise from top left: Potted cheese; Hundreds and thousands pâté; Finnan cocottes; Shrimp puffs.

POTTED CHEESE

Serves 4-6

¼ cup curd cheese
1½ cups Cheddar cheese, grated
⅓ cup blue cheese, crumbled
4 tablespoons plain unsweetened yogurt
2 tablespoons medium sherry
freshly ground black pepper
1 tablespoon chopped parsley
bay leaves or parsley sprigs, to garnish
whole wheat bread slices

Preparation time: 20 minutes

1. Beat the curd cheese until it is soft. Beat in the cheeses and yogurt and then the sherry, a few drops at a time. Season with pepper and stir in the parsley.
2. Spoon the cheese into a serving bowl or individual dishes and level the top. Cover the dish and chill. ⅎ Garnish with bay leaves or parsley sprigs.
3. Using cookie cutters, cut the bread into hearts or other decorative shapes. Toast the shapes and serve with the potted cheese.

ⅎ *Freeze the potted cheese for up to 1 month. Thaw in the refrigerator for 3-4 hours.*

HUNDREDS AND THOUSANDS PÂTÉ

Serves 6-8

½ lb smoked cod's roe
1 cup curd cheese
2 tablespoons lemon juice
1 hard-cooked egg, finely chopped
1 tablespoon sunflower oil
freshly ground black pepper
8 tablespoons condensed consommé
1 tablespoon medium sherry
1 teaspoon powdered gelatin
To garnish:
· chervil leaves
red and black lumpfish roe

*Preparation time: 30 minutes, plus setting
Cooking time: 3 minutes*

1. Put the cod's roe in a bowl and pour on boiling water to cover. Drain the roe, cool slightly and peel off the skin. Mash the roe to break it up.
2. Mix together the roe, cheese, lemon juice, chopped egg and sunflower oil and beat well. Taste and season the mixture with pepper, then spoon into a serving dish.
3. Heat the consommé with the sherry, stir in the gelatin and dissolve. Set aside to cool.
4. When the gelatin mixture is like unbeaten egg white, spoon it over the pâté. Cover and put in the refrigerator to set.
5. Garnish the pâté with the herbs and the red and black lumpfish roe arranged like bunches of grapes.

FINNAN COCOTTES

Serves 4

½ lb smoked haddock fillet
2 bay leaves
6 black peppercorns
1 cup cottage cheese
3 scallions, chopped
1 cup mushrooms, chopped
2 eggs, beaten
1 tablespoon lemon juice
salt
freshly ground black pepper
3 tablespoons fresh whole wheat breadcrumbs
1 tablespoon grated Parmesan cheese
1 teaspoon paprika
4 lemon slices, to garnish, (optional)

*Preparation time: 15 minutes
Cooking time: 45 minutes
Oven: 350°F*

1. Place the fish in a pan with the bay leaves, peppercorns and just enough water to cover. Bring to the boil and simmer for 5 minutes. Drain, cool and flake the fish, removing the skin and any bones.
2. Mix the fish with the cottage cheese, scallions and mushrooms. Stir in the beaten eggs and lemon juice and season with salt and pepper.
3. Divide the mixture between 4 greased cocotte dishes and level the tops. Mix together the breadcrumbs, cheese and paprika and sprinkle on top of each dish.
4. Stand the dishes in a roasting pan with water to come half-way up the sides. Cook in a preheated oven for 35 minutes, or until the mixture is just firm.
5. Serve hot, garnished with lemon slices, if liked, and accompanied by hot toast.

SPICED FISH CAKES

Serves 4

1 lb fillets of white fish, skinned
1¼ cups skim milk
1 bay leaf
2 tablespoons low fat margarine
1 small onion, peeled and finely chopped
1 green pepper, seeded, cored and finely chopped
½ teaspoon chili powder, or to taste
¼ cup whole wheat flour
salt
1 egg, beaten
5 tablespoons whole wheat breadcrumbs
½ cup peanuts, crushed or finely chopped
1 tablespoon milk
2 tablespoons sunflower oil
celery stalk, to garnish
Sauce:
3 scallions, finely chopped
2½ tablespoons chopped mint
1¼ teaspoons lemon juice
⅔ cup plain unsweetened yogurt, chilled

Preparation time: 25 minutes
Cooking time: 15 minutes

1. Poach the fish in the milk with the bay leaf for 10 minutes, turning it once. Allow to cool slightly. Drain and chop the fish and reserve the milk.
2. Meanwhile, make the sauce. Beat the scallions, mint and lemon juice into the yogurt. Chill in the refrigerator.
3. Melt the low fat margarine and fry the onion and pepper over medium heat for 3 minutes, stirring once or twice. Stir in the chili powder and cook for 1 minute. Stir in the flour. Pour on the reserved milk, stirring constantly until the sauce boils. Simmer for 3 minutes. Beat the sauce thoroughly.
4. Remove from the heat, beat in the fish and season with salt. Beat in half the egg. Leave the mixture to cool, then shape into 8 flat cakes. Mix together the breadcrumbs and the finely chopped peanuts.
5. Beat the remaining egg with the tablespoon of milk. Dip the fish cakes in the egg mixture and then in the breadcrumbs and peanuts, to coat. Heat the oil in a non-stick skillet and fry the cakes for 3-4 minutes on each side.
6. Garnish with a celery stalk and serve hot with the chilled sauce.

GOLDEN SALAD

Serves 4

4 smoked mackerel fillets
2 large oranges, peeled and divided into segments
2 apples, cored and thinly sliced
2 tender celery stalks, thinly sliced
2½ tablespoons walnut halves
ruffled endive or lettuce leaves
4 thin orange slices, to garnish
Dressing:
1¼ teaspoons grated orange rind
4 tablespoons orange juice
2½ tablespoons tomato juice
a large pinch cayenne pepper
freshly ground black pepper
1¼ tablespoons light honey
2½ tablespoons finely chopped chives

Preparation time: 20 minutes

1. Skin the mackerel fillets and slice each one into 4 pieces.
2. Mix together the dressing ingredients.

3. Toss the oranges, apples, celery and walnuts in the dressing. Carefully stir in the mackerel.
4. Line a plate with salad leaves and spoon on the salad. Garnish with the orange slices.

VINEYARD PARCELS

Serves 6

¼ cup dried apricots, soaked, drained and chopped
½ cup cooked brown rice
1 cup seedless raisins, chopped
½ cup blanched almonds, chopped
1 cooking apple, peeled, cored and finely chopped
1¼ teaspoons grated orange rind
4 tablespoons orange juice
2½ tablespoons light honey
1 lb grape leaves, well rinsed and drained
Sauce:
4 tablespoons orange juice
⅔ cup chicken stock

Preparation time: 1 hour
Cooking time: 50 minutes
Oven: 350°F

1. Mix together the apricots, rice, raisins, almonds, apple, orange rind and orange juice and the honey.
2. Spread 24 of the vine leaves out flat, stalk side towards you. Place a spoonful of the filling in the center of each leaf. Roll up from the base, fold over the sides and wrap into a tight, neat parcel.
3. Cover a shallow baking dish with a layer of the remaining vine leaves and arrange the parcels in a single layer on top.
4. To make the sauce, mix together the orange juice and stock. Pour the sauce over the vine leaf parcels. Cover with any remaining leaves and cover the dish with foil. Cook in a preheated oven for 50 minutes. Remove the foil and serve hot.

From the left: Spiced fish cakes; Vineyard parcels; Golden salad.

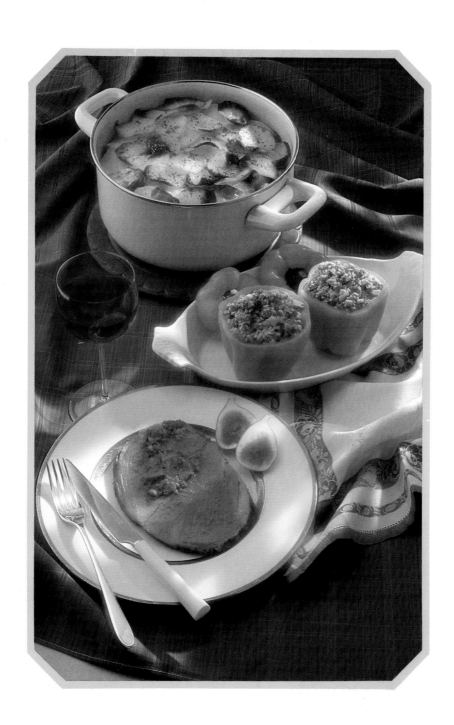

MEAT, POULTRY & GAME

Many people confuse wholefood cooking with a vegetarian diet and so, if they enjoy meat and fish dishes, they close their minds to the whole subject. This is a great pity as wholefood cooking embraces all natural and unadulterated ingredients, including high-protein foods such as meat and fish. However wholefood menus do tend to rely less on animal proteins, often to the extent of using a little meat in the Chinese way to complement and flavor grains and pasta, rather than as the main and predominant ingredient.

To prepare and cook meat in the most healthy way it is important to eliminate as much as possible of the visible and hidden fat. This means trimming off the fat you can see on chops, steak and so on, and frying cubed meat for casseroles in the very minimum of oil or – if you have a non-stick skillet – none at all. If you dry-fry the meat in this way, you can discard the melted fat – and many of the calories – before proceeding with the dish. Remember, too, that poultry is better for you than red meat since its fat content is less, particularly if you remove the skin before cooking, and that birds and meat from animals that have not been force fed or fattened with drugs have the best flavor.

ROLLED BEEF

Serves 4

4 'minute' steaks, about 5 oz each
1½ tablespoons butter
2½ tablespoons sunflower oil
1¼ tablespoons chopped parsley, to garnish
Filling:
½ lb frozen spinach, thawed and well drained
¾ cup curd cheese
½ cup small mushrooms, chopped
salt
freshly ground black pepper
pinch of grated nutmeg
Sauce:
1¼ tablespoons sunflower oil
1 medium onion, peeled and finely chopped
1 garlic clove, peeled and crushed
2½ tablespoons tomato paste
1 lb tomatoes, skinned and sliced
7½ tablespoons chicken or beef stock
1¼ teaspoons dried oregano
¾ teaspoon grated orange rind

Preparation time: 30 minutes
Cooking time: 1¼ hours
Oven: 350°F

1. To make the sauce, heat the oil in a small pan and fry the onion over moderate heat for 3 minutes. Add the garlic and tomato paste, the tomatoes, stock, oregano and orange rind and season with salt and pepper. Bring to the boil, uncovered, and simmer for 20 minutes.
2. To make the filling, beat the spinach and cheese and stir in the mushrooms. Season with salt, pepper and nutmeg.
3. Place each steak flat on the table. Spread with the filling and roll up, jelly-roll style. Tie each roll in 2 places with string.
4. Heat the butter and oil in a flameproof casserole and fry the beef rolls over moderate heat for 5-6 minutes, turning them to brown evenly.
5. Pour the sauce over the meat, cover and cook in a preheated oven for 40-50 minutes.
6. Taste the sauce and adjust the seasoning if necessary. Remove the strings. Serve the dish garnished with the parsley.

Clockwise from top left: Rolled beef; Jugged beef; Rickshaw lamb.

RICKSHAW LAMB

Serves 6

3 lb loin of lamb, boned and layer of fat and skin removed
1 cup brown short-grain rice
freshly ground black pepper
Marinade:
1¼ tablespoons grated orange rind
4 tablespoons orange juice
1 large onion, peeled and sliced
2½ tablespoons sunflower oil
2½ tablespoons soy sauce
2½ tablespoons light honey
6 tablespoons cider
1¼ teaspoons ground cinnamon

Preparation time: 30 minutes, plus marinating
Cooking time: 1¼ hours
Oven: 375°F

JUGGED BEEF

Serves 4

2¼ lb beef foreshank, cut across the bone into
1 inch slices
3 tablespoons flour
salt
freshly ground black pepper
1 teaspoon grated orange rind
3 tablespoons sunflower oil
1½ tablespoons butter
2 large onions, peeled and thinly sliced
12 oz carrots, scraped and thinly sliced
2 garlic cloves, peeled and crushed
2 bay leaves
1¼ cups red wine

Preparation time: 30 minutes
Cooking time: 2½ hours
Oven: 250°F

The dish is improved if it is made the day before serving. When it is completely cold, lift off the layer of fat on top.

1. Toss the meat in the flour seasoned with the salt, pepper and orange rind.
2. Heat the oil and butter in a flameproof casserole. Fry the onions and carrots for 4-5 minutes over a moderate heat, stirring frequently, until they are just beginning to brown. Remove them with a slotted spoon and set them on one side.
3. Fry the meat gently until it is evenly browned on all sides.
4. Return the onions and carrots to the casserole, and add the garlic, bay leaves and wine. Stir well and bring to the boil.
5. Cover the casserole and cook in a preheated oven for 2 hours, or until the meat is tender. Taste and adjust the seasoning if necessary. Discard the bay leaves and skim off any fat that has risen to the surface. **F**

F *Freeze for up to 3 months. Thaw in the refrigerator overnight. Heat on top of the cooker until bubbling.*

1. Mix together all the marinade ingredients. Put the marinade into a strong polythene bag, add the lamb and tie the bag securely. Shake it to cover the meat on all sides. Place the bag on a plate and leave in the refrigerator for several hours or overnight. Turn the bag occasionally, if possible.
2. Drain the lamb, reserving the marinade. Put the lamb in a roasting pan, pour on 2 tablespoons of the marinade and 2 tablespoons of water and cover with foil. Bake in a preheated oven for 45 minutes. Remove the foil, baste the meat and cook for a further 30 minutes.
3. While the meat is cooking, put the rice in a pan. Measure the marinade, make it up to 2½ cups with water and season with pepper. Bring to the boil, pour over the rice, cover the pan and simmer for 45 minutes, stirring occasionally.
4. Transfer the meat to a heated serving dish and surround it with the rice.

VEGETABLE AND BARLEY HOTPOT

Serves 4

1 cup pearl barley, soaked
9 bacon slices, rinded, cut into squares
2 large onions, peeled and chopped
1 garlic clove, peeled and crushed
6 celery stalks, thinly sliced
2 medium zucchini, thinly sliced
12 oz carrots, scraped and thinly sliced
2 cups small mushrooms, sliced
2½ cups chicken stock
4 tablespoons chopped parsley
1 tablespoon tomato paste
salt
freshly ground black pepper
1 tablespoon soy sauce

Preparation time: 20 minutes
Cooking time: 2¼ hours
Oven: 350°F

1. Cook the barley in boiling water for 1 hour. Drain.
2. Fry the bacon in a flameproof casserole over moderate heat until it is crisp. Remove with a slotted spoon and set aside. Discard all but 2 tablespoons of fat in the casserole.
3. Fry the onions, garlic and celery for 2 minutes. Add the zucchini, carrots and mushrooms. Pour on the stock and stir in the barley and bacon. Stir in 3 tablespoons of the parsley, the tomato paste, salt, pepper and soy sauce and bring to the boil.
4. Cover the casserole and cook in a preheated oven for 1 hour. Taste and adjust the seasoning. Sprinkle on the remaining parsley and serve hot.

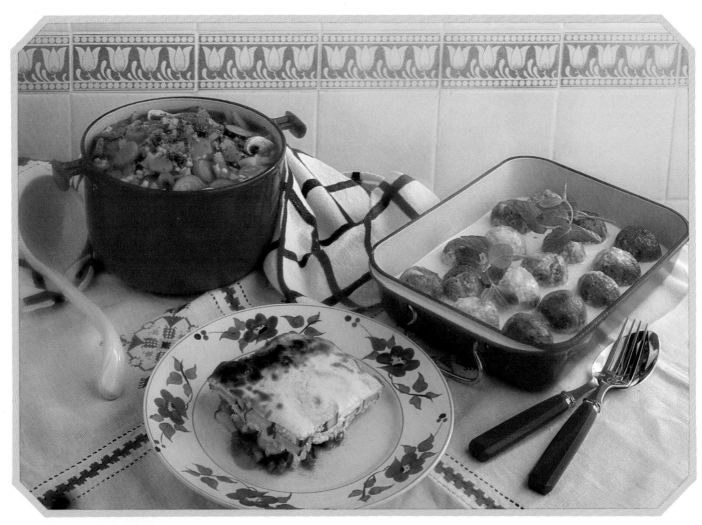

ZUCCHINI LAYER PIE

Serves 4

5 tablespoons sunflower oil
1 lb zucchini, sliced
8 oz onions, peeled and thinly sliced
1 lb ground lean beef
1 lb tomatoes, peeled and sliced
¾ teaspoon dried oregano
2½ tablespoons chopped parsley
salt
freshly ground black pepper
3 oz cheese, very thinly sliced
Topping:
1¼ cups plain unsweetened yogurt
2 eggs
pinch of grated nutmeg
½ cup cheese, grated

Preparation time: 30 minutes
Cooking time: 1¼ hours
Oven: 375°F

1. Heat 4 tablespoons of the oil in a large skillet pan and fry the zucchini for about 2 minutes on each side over moderately high heat, until they begin to brown. Remove the zucchini and set aside.

2. Heat the remaining oil and fry the onions over moderate heat for 3 minutes. Add the meat and fry gently for 5 minutes, stirring often.

3. Add the tomatoes, oregano and parsley and season with salt and pepper. Bring to the boil, cover the pan and simmer for 10 minutes, stirring occasionally.

4. In a shallow, greased baking dish, make layers of the meat sauce, zucchini and cheese slices.

5. To make the topping, beat together the yogurt, eggs, nutmeg and grated cheese and pour over the dish.

6. Bake in a preheated oven for 1 hour, until the topping is deep brown. ☒ Serve hot.

☒ *Cool the dish, cover and freeze for up to 3 months. Reheat from frozen in the oven at 350°F for about 1¼ hours.*

BEEF AND RAISIN MEATBALLS

Serves 4

1 lb ground lean beef
1 small onion, peeled and finely chopped
2½ tablespoons seedless raisins, chopped
2½ tablespoons walnuts, chopped
2½ tablespoons chopped parsley
½ teaspoon ground allspice
salt
freshly ground black pepper
1 egg, beaten
flour, for dusting
mint sprigs, to garnish
Sauce:
1¼ cups plain unsweetened yogurt
1¼ teaspoons lemon juice

Preparation time: 20 minutes
Cooking time: 45 minutes

1. Purée the beef in a blender or food processor until it is a smooth paste. Beat in the onion, raisins, walnuts, parsley and spice, season with salt and pepper and beat in just enough of the egg to bind the mixture to a firm paste.

2. Flour your hands and shape the mixture into rounds almost the size of golf balls. ☒

3. Place the meatballs in a single layer in a flameproof casserole. Pour on the yogurt and lemon juice and season with salt and pepper.

4. Cover the dish and simmer for 45 minutes. Serve garnished with the mint sprigs.

☒ *Open-freeze the meat balls, then transfer them to a rigid container and freeze for up to 1 month. Thaw in the refrigerator for 3-4 hours or at room temperature for 2-3 hours.*

Clockwise from top left: Vegetable and barley hotpot; Beef and raisin meatballs; Zucchini layer pie.

LAMB AND VEGETABLE COUSCOUS

Serves 6

1 lb medium couscous (from Middle Eastern foodstores)
salt
2½ tablespoons sunflower oil
2¼ lb lean leg of lamb, trimmed of excess fat and cut into 2 inch cubes
12 pearl onions or shallots, peeled
1 teaspoon chili powder
1 teaspoon ground coriander
1¼ tablespoons tomato paste
1 lb tomatoes, peeled and sliced
about 1¼ cups beef stock (see page 11)
2 medium carrots, scraped and sliced
2 medium potatoes, peeled and diced
1 cup frozen peas
1 cup frozen snap beans
2½ tablespoons chopped coriander leaves, or parsley, to garnish.

Preparation time: 45 minutes
Cooking time: 2¼ hours

Couscous is produced from the semolina made from hard durum wheat. The semolina grains are moistened, coated with flour and 'expanded' to produce light and fluffy cereal grains. They are cooked by steaming for about 45-50 minutes, either over fast-boiling water or, as in this typically Algerian recipe, partly over water and partly – for added flavour – over a meat or fish stew.

1. Rinse the couscous in a strainer under cold, running water. Fork over the grains to break up any lumps. Fit a steamer or colander lined with a double-thickness of clean dish towel over a pan of boiling water. Add the couscous a little at a time, forking it through all the while. Season with salt and steam, uncovered, for 30 minutes.

2. Turn the couscous into a large bowl and pour on 2 cups cold water. Mix well with a fork and set aside.

3. Heat the oil in a large pan, or the base of the steamer, and fry the lamb over moderate heat, stirring it to brown evenly. Stir in the onions, chili powder and coriander and cook for 1 minute. Stir in the tomato paste, tomatoes and stock and bring to the boil.

4. Cover the pan and simmer for 1 hour.

5. Add the carrots and potatoes, cover and continue simmering for 15 minutes.

6. Add the peas and beans. Place the steamer or the colander lined with a dish towel on the pan. Place the couscous grains in the top, cover with a lid or foil and continue cooking for 15 minutes. Fluff up the grains with a fork from time to time.

7. Spoon the meat and vegetables into the center of a heated serving dish and arrange the couscous in a ring around the outside. Garnish with the chopped coriander.

Below: Lamb and vegetable couscous.
Right: Lamb in pepper cases.

LAMB IN PEPPER CASES

Serves 4

4 large green and yellow peppers
salt
2 tablespoons sunflower oil
8 oz lean ground lamb
1 medium onion, finely chopped
½ cup mushrooms, finely chopped
freshly ground black pepper
¾ cup whole wheat breadcrumbs
1 teaspoon grated lemon rind
1 teaspoon lemon juice
2 tablespoons chopped parsley
2 tablespoons chopped blanched almonds
4 tablespoons plain unsweetened yogurt

Preparation time: 20 minutes
Cooking time: 1¼ hours
Oven: 375°F

1. Cut the tops from the peppers and set them aside. Scoop out the core and seeds.
2. Blanch the peppers and the tops in boiling, salted water for 5 minutes. Drain well.
3. Heat the oil in a pan and fry the meat over a moderate heat for 4-5 minutes, stirring frequently. Remove it with a slotted spoon. Fry the onion and mushrooms for 3 minutes, stirring once or twice. Return the meat to the pan and simmer, uncovered, for 15 minutes, stirring often.
4. Remove from the heat, season with salt and pepper and stir in the breadcrumbs, lemon rind, lemon juice, parsley, almonds and yogurt. Mix well.
5. Stand the peppers upright in a baking dish that just fits them. Fill them with the meat mixture and replace the lids.
6. Pour 2 inches of water into the dish, cover with foil and bake in a preheated oven for 50 minutes. Remove the foil 15 minutes before the end. Serve the peppers hot, with brown rice.

CASSOULET

Serves 8-10

3½ lb roasting chicken
1 lb dried navy beans, soaked overnight
and drained
2 bay leaves
2 large onions, peeled and sliced
2-3 garlic cloves, crushed
1 bouquet garni
2 medium carrots, scraped and thinly sliced
2¼ lb lean lamb, cut into fingers
4 celery stalks, thinly sliced
1 lb tomatoes, skinned and sliced
3 tablespoons tomato paste
1 teaspoon whole grain mustard
salt
freshly ground black pepper
2 tablespoons chopped parsley
1 tablespoon chopped parsley, to garnish

Preparation time: 45 minutes
Cooking time: 5 hours
Oven: 300°F

1. Put the chicken and beans in a large pan with the bay leaves, 1 sliced onion, the garlic and the bouquet garni. Cover with water, bring to the boil, cover the pan and boil for 10 minutes. Lower the heat and simmer for 1 hour.
2. Drain the chicken and beans, reserving the stock. Cut the flesh from the bones. Discard the bouquet garni and bay leaves.
3. In a large casserole, make layers of the chicken, beans, remaining onion, carrots, lamb, celery and tomatoes. Mix together the tomato paste, mustard and 4½ cups of the reserved stock, season with salt and pepper and stir in the parsley.
4. Pour the stock into the casserole and cook, uncovered, in a preheated oven for 3 hours. F
5. Add a little more hot stock, if necessary with the parsley sprigs and return to the oven for 45 minutes.

F *This is a dish that freezes particularly well, and is good to have made in advance for an informal party. Freeze for up to 3 months. Thaw at room temperature for about 12 hours.*

From the top: Cassoulet; Loin of lamb Victoria.

LOIN OF LAMB VICTORIA

Serves 4

1½ tablespoons soft margarine
1 small onion, peeled and finely chopped
1½ tablespoons chopped parsley
1½ cups whole wheat breadcrumbs
8 oz sweet plums, stoned and chopped, plus 2
for garnish
1 large cooking apple, peeled, cored and chopped
salt
freshly ground black pepper
½ teaspoon ground coriander
3 tablespoons orange juice
2¼ lb loin of lamb, boned
parsley sprigs, to garnish
Sauce:
1 tablespoon flour
1¼ cups chicken stock
2 tablespoons port
2 tablespoons redcurrant jelly

Preparation time: 30 minutes
Cooking time: 1 hour 20 minutes
Oven: 375°F

1. Melt the margarine in a pan and fry the onion over moderate heat for 3 minutes, stirring once or twice.
2. Remove the pan from the heat and stir in the parsley, breadcrumbs, plums and apple and season with salt, pepper and coriander. Stir in the orange juice and mix well. F
3. Spoon the filling into the cavity in the meat, roll it neatly and tie with string.
4. Place the meat in a roasting pan and cook in a preheated oven for 1-1¼ hours, until it is cooked to your liking.
5. Transfer the meat to a heated serving dish, cover with foil and keep warm. Pour off all but 1 tablespoon of the fat.
6. Over a moderate heat, stir in the flour. Pour on the stock, stirring constantly. Add the port and redcurrant jelly and season with salt and pepper. Bring to the boil and simmer for 3 minutes. Strain the sauce and serve it separately.
7. Stone and quarter the plums and use them with the parsley sprigs to garnish the meat.

F *You can freeze the stuffing separately in a rigid container for up to 1 month or freeze the uncooked, boned and rolled joint for up to 3 months. Thaw overnight in the refrigerator.*

BOSPHORUS LAMB WITH FIGS

Serves 4

2¾-3 lb leg of lamb, boned
sliced, fresh figs, to garnish
Filling:
5 oz dried figs, chopped
1 cup fresh whole wheat breadcrumbs
1 small onion, peeled and finely chopped
1 teaspoon grated orange rind
3 tablespoons orange juice
¼ teaspoon ground cinnamon
salt
freshly ground black pepper

Preparation time: 25 minutes
Cooking time: about 1½ hours
Oven: 375°F

1. Mix together all the ingredients for the filling.
2. Press the filling into the cavity in the meat, close it to make a neat shape and tie with string.
3. Place the meat on a wire rack in a roasting pan and cook in a preheated oven for 1½ hours, or until the meat is cooked to your liking.
4. Remove the strings, transfer the meat to a heated serving dish and garnish the dish with the sliced figs.

GALWAY STEW

Serves 4

2¼ lb potatoes, peeled and sliced
3½ lb neck lamb chops, trimmed of excess fat
1 lb onions, peeled and sliced
4 leeks, white part only, sliced
salt
freshly ground black pepper
2½ tablespoons chopped parsley
1¼ teaspoons dried thyme
2 cups chicken stock
1¼ tablespoons tomato paste
1¼ tablespoons chopped parsley, to garnish

Preparation time: 20 minutes
Cooking time: 3 hours
Oven: 275°F

1. In a large casserole, make layers of potatoes, lamb chops, onions and leeks, seasoning with salt and pepper and sprinkling parsley and thyme between each layer. Begin and end with a layer of potatoes, overlapping the potato slices in neat rings to form the 'crust'.
2. Mix together the stock and tomato paste and pour into the casserole.
3. Cover the dish with a layer of foil and the lid. Cook in a preheated oven for 2 hours. Remove the foil and lid and add a little more stock or water if needed.
4. Return the dish to the oven, uncovered, for a further 1 hour, to brown the potatoes. Sprinkle with chopped parsley and serve with a green vegetable and plenty of whole wheat bread.

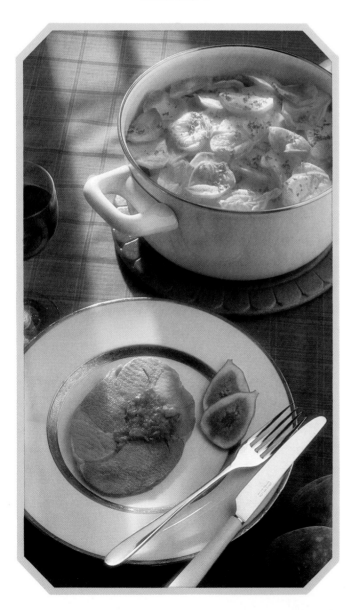

Left, from the top: Galway stew; Bosphorus lamb with figs.
Right, from the top: Mushrooms and liver provençal; Stir-fried pork and cashews.

1. Toss the liver slices in the flour seasoned with the salt, pepper and marjoram.
2. Melt the margarine and oil in a skillet and fry the liver for 2 minutes on each side over a moderate heat. Remove the liver.
3. Fry the garlic, onion, peppers and mushrooms for 2 minutes, stirring. Add the tomatoes, sugar and vinegar. Stir well and return the liver to the skillet.
4. Cover the skillet and simmer for 10-15 minutes.
5. While the liver is cooking, cook the noodles in boiling, salted water for 10 minutes, or according to the instructions on the packet, until tender.

STIR-FRIED PORK AND CASHEWS

Serves 4

4 tablespoons sunflower oil
1 lb pork fillet, trimmed and cut into
¼ inch strips
1 garlic clove, peeled and crushed
1 slice ginger root, peeled and
finely chopped
6 scallions, sliced
1 cup cashew nuts
1 red pepper, cored, seeded and thinly sliced
4 oz bean-sprouts
Sauce:
1 tablespoon cornstarch
5 tablespoons chicken stock
5 tablespoons dry sherry
1 tablespoon soy sauce
freshly ground black pepper

Preparation time: 20 minutes
Cooking time: 10 minutes

1. To make the sauce, put the cornstarch into a bowl, pour on the chicken stock and stir it to a paste. Stir in the sherry, orange juice and soy sauce and season with pepper.
2. Heat 2 tablespoons of the oil in a heavy skillet or wok. Add the strips of pork and stir-fry over high heat for 2-3 minutes. Remove the meat and keep warm.
3. Heat the remaining oil and stir-fry the garlic, ginger, scallions and nuts for 2 minutes. Add the red pepper and bean-sprouts and stir-fry for a further 2 minutes.
4. Return the pork to the pan, pour on the sauce, bring to the boil, stirring, lower the heat and simmer for 2 minutes.

MUSHROOMS AND LIVER PROVENÇAL

Serves 4

1 lb lamb's liver, sliced
4 tablespoons whole wheat flour
salt
freshly ground black pepper
1¼ teaspoons fresh marjoram
2 tablespoons margarine
1¼ tablespoons sunflower oil
1 garlic clove, peeled and crushed
1 medium onion, peeled and thinly sliced
1 green pepper, cored, seeded and sliced
1 red pepper, cored, seeded and sliced
1 cup mushrooms, sliced
4 large tomatoes, skinned and sliced
2½ teaspoons soft dark brown sugar
1¼ teaspoons red wine vinegar
12 oz dried green tagliatelle

Preparation time: 15 minutes
Cooking time: 20 minutes

VEAL KEBABS WITH GINGER DRESSING

Serves 4

1 lb hindshank veal, trimmed of excess fat and cut into 1 inch cubes
1 green pepper, cored, seeded and cut into 1 inch squares
1 red pepper, cored, seeded and cut into 1 inch squares
2 medium zucchini, cut into ½ inch slices
1 cup tiny mushrooms
4 bay leaves
1 lemon or orange, quartered, to garnish
Marinade:
3 tablespoons sunflower oil
1 tablespoon red wine vinegar
2 teaspoons grated orange rind
1 tablespoon orange juice
1 inch piece fresh root ginger, peeled and chopped
½ teaspoon ground ginger
salt
freshly ground black pepper

Preparation time: 25 minutes, plus marinating
Cooking time: 15 minutes

1. Mix together the marinade ingredients.
2. On 4 skewers, thread the veal, peppers, zucchini, mushrooms and bay leaves, alternating the colours and ending with a bay leaf.
3. Place the skewers in a shallow dish, pour over the marinade and turn the skewers in the mixture. Cover and set aside for about 2 hours.
4. Heat the broiler to moderate. Drain the skewers and broil for 10-12 minutes, turning frequently and basting them with the marinade. Garnish with the lemon or orange wedges. Serve immediately with brown rice.

VEAL WITH CHILI

Serves 4

8 oz red kidney beans, soaked overnight and drained
1 small onion, peeled and sliced
1 bay leaf
1 bouquet garni
1 tablespoon sunflower oil
2 medium onions, peeled and sliced
1 garlic clove, peeled and finely chopped
1 lb ground veal shoulder
1 tablespoon whole wheat flour
salt
freshly ground black pepper
1 teaspoon dried oregano
1 teaspoon paprika
1 teaspoon chili powder (or to taste)
2 red peppers, cored, seeded and thinly sliced
12 oz tomatoes, skinned and sliced
1¼ cups chicken stock

Preparation time: 20 minutes, plus soaking overnight
Cooking time: 2 hours

1. Put the kidney beans, onion, bay leaf and bouquet garni into a pan, cover with water, bring to the boil and fast-boil for 15-20 minutes. Lower the heat and simmer for 1 hour. Drain. Remove the bouquet garni and the bay leaf.

2. Heat the oil in a flameproof casserole and fry the onion and garlic over a moderate heat for 2 minutes, stirring once or twice. Add the meat, stir well and cook for 5 minutes. Stir in the flour, salt, pepper, oregano, paprika and chili powder and cook for 2 minutes. Add the peppers, tomatoes and kidney bean mixture and pour on the stock.

3. Bring to the boil, cover the dish and simmer for 45 minutes, 'stirring occasionally. Taste and adjust the seasoning if necessary. **F**

F *Freeze the dish for up to 2 months. Thaw from frozen in a pan on top of the cooker.*

RED PEPPER CHICKEN

Serves 4

4 chicken breasts, skinned
2 tablespoons soft margarine
2½ tablespoons sunflower oil
12 black olives, to garnish
Sauce:
1¼ tablespoons sunflower oil
1 medium onion, peeled and finely chopped
2 garlic cloves, peeled and finely chopped
2 red peppers, cored, seeded and thinly sliced
1 lb tomatoes, skinned and sliced
1¼ tablespoons tomato paste
2½ teaspoons red wine vinegar
5 tablespoons Spanish olives, sliced
1½ teaspoons soft dark brown sugar
salt
freshly ground black pepper
pinch of ground cumin
2½ tablespoons chopped parsley

Preparation time: 20 minutes
Cooking time: 50 minutes

1. Dry the chicken breasts on paper towels. Heat the margarine and oil in a skillet and fry the chicken over a moderate heat for 5 minutes on each side. Remove the chicken from the skillet and keep it warm.

2. To make the sauce, heat the oil in the skillet and fry the onion and garlic over a moderate heat for 3 minutes, stirring once or twice. Add the peppers and cook for 2 minutes. Then add the tomatoes, tomato paste, vinegar, olives and sugar and season well with salt, pepper and cumin. Bring the sauce to the boil and simmer, uncovered, for 15 minutes.

3. Return the chicken to the pan and simmer for 15-20 minutes, until it is cooked. Stir in the parsley, taste the sauce and adjust the seasoning if needed.

4. Garnish the dish with the black olives. This dish is good served with whole wheat pasta shells or rice, and a green salad.

From the left: Veal kebabs with ginger dressing; Veal with chili; Red pepper chicken.

CHICKEN IN A BRICK

Serves 4-6

3¼ lb roasting chicken
1¼ tablespoons lemon juice
Filling:
2 tablespoons margarine
1 small onion, peeled and finely chopped
1 celery stalk, finely chopped
½ cup dried pears, chopped
1 cup fresh whole wheat breadcrumbs
½ cup Brazil nuts, chopped
1¼ teaspoons grated lemon rind
salt
freshly ground black pepper
1 small egg, beaten
parsley sprigs, to garnish

Preparation time: 35 minutes
Cooking time: 1 hour 50 minutes
Oven: 425°F (do not preheat)

Although a chicken brick is used in this recipe, you can, of course, cook the chicken with dried pear stuffing in a roasting pan in the oven in the normal way.

1. Soak the chicken brick in warm water for 15 minutes. To make the filling, melt the margarine and fry the onion and celery together over moderate heat for 3 minutes, stirring once or twice. Remove from the heat and stir in the pears, breadcrumbs, Brazil nuts and lemon rind and season with salt and pepper. Beat in the egg. **F**
2. Wipe the chicken inside and out with a damp cloth. Spoon the filling into the cavity and tie the legs together with string. Sprinkle the lemon juice over the bird.
3. Line the chicken brick with waxed paper. Place the bird in the brick, cover with waxed paper and put on the lid.
4. Place the chicken brick in a cold oven and set the heat as indicated. Cook for 1¾ hours, or until the chicken is cooked. To test, pierce the thickest part of the thigh with a fine skewer: the juices should run clear.
5. Transfer the chicken to a heated serving dish and garnish with parsley sprigs. Pour off the juices from the brick and serve separately.

F *Freeze the filling for up to 1 month. Thaw completely before using.*

ALMOND-COATED TURKEY

Serves 4

4 turkey breast slices, about 4-5 oz each
½ cup chopped blanched almonds
2 oz soft margarine
1¼ tablespoons sunflower oil
2½ teaspoons whole wheat flour
⅔ cup plain unsweetened yogurt
2½ tablespoons chicken stock
1¼ tablespoons grated orange rind
5 tablespoons orange juice
salt
freshly ground black pepper
pinch of ground cinnamon
2 oranges, segmented, to garnish

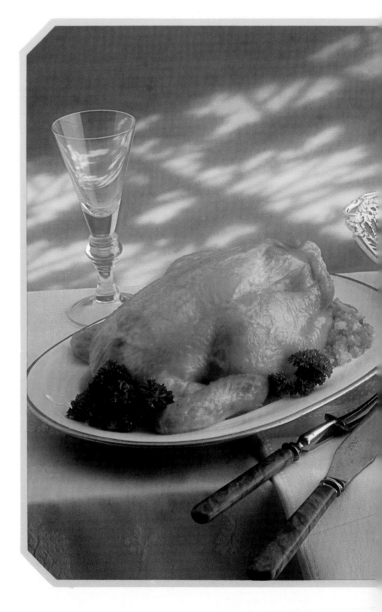

Preparation time: 15 minutes
Cooking time: 15 minutes

1. Coat the turkey in the chopped almonds, pressing the nuts well into the meat.
2. Heat the margarine and oil in a skillet and fry the turkey slices over a moderate heat for 5 minutes on each side. Remove them from the pan and keep them warm.
3. In a small pan, stir the flour to a paste with a little of the yogurt, then pour on the remainder and bring to the boil, stirring. Simmer for 3 minutes.
4. Stir the stock, orange rind and juice into the frying pan and bring to the boil. Pour on the yogurt, season with salt, pepper and cinnamon and simmer for 1 minute.
5. Pour the sauce on to a heated serving dish. Place the turkey slices on the sauce and garnish with the orange segments.

RABBIT WITH JUNIPER

Serves 4

2¼ lb rabbit pieces
1½ tablespoons margarine
2½ tablespoons sunflower oil
⅔ cup cider
⅔ cup plain unsweetened yogurt
2½ teaspoons whole wheat flour
1½ tablespoons chopped parsley, to garnish
Marinade:
2½ tablespoons sunflower oil
⅔ cup red wine
10 juniper berries, crushed
strip of thinly pared orange rind
salt
freshly ground black pepper
1 small onion, peeled and sliced
2 bay leaves

Preparation time: 40 minutes, plus marinating
Cooking time: 1¼ hours

1. Mix together the marinade ingredients. Pour the marinade into a strong plastic bag and add the rabbit pieces. Tie the bag securely, turn it from side to side and place it on a plate. Leave in the refrigerator for at least 4 hours, or overnight.
2. Strain the rabbit, reserving the marinade. Cut the flesh from the bones and dry the meat on paper towels.
3. Heat the margarine and oil in a flameproof casserole. Fry the rabbit over a moderate heat until it is evenly browned on all sides. Pour on the strained marinade and the cider, season with salt and pepper and bring to the boil.
4. Cover the casserole and simmer gently for 45 minutes.
5. Pour a little of the yogurt on to the flour, stirring constantly, then stir in the remainder. In a small pan, bring the yogurt to the boil, stirring, and simmer for 3 minutes.
6. Stir the yogurt into the casserole and simmer for 15 minutes, or until the meat is tender. Garnish the dish with the parsley. Serve with rice or noodles.

Clockwise from the left: Chicken in a brick; Rabbit with juniper; Almond-coated turkey.

FISH DISHES

Fish of all kinds is the perfect wholefood. It is high in protein and packed with minerals and vitamins, yet relatively low – in comparison with meat – in both fat and calories, and so deserves equally high ranking as a main-dish ingredient. Fish farms apart, it is the only true wild fresh food that we have. It is also easier to digest than meat and, generally, it does not take so long to cook.

The more oily fish, such as herring, mackerel, trout and sardines are well complemented, as our recipes show, by fruit, vegetables, spices and fibre. Baked apple trout has an apple filling, Baked herrings in ginger sauce, a piquant Chinese-inspired sauce, whilst Mackerel with oranges combines fruit, vegetables and fibre in its stuffing of oranges, celery, scallions and brown rice.

White fish combines particularly well with high-fibre foods, too. A fish pie takes on a new personality when the piecrust consists of crisp and crunchy whole wheat pastry, and both creamy fish soufflés and rolled fillets are given added flavour, 'bite' and valuable dietary fibre with the addition of corn, the ingredient New Englanders selected as the best complement to their sea harvest.

TROUT VINAIGRETTE

Serves 4

4 tablespoons soft margarine
1 large onion, peeled and thinly sliced into rings
1 green pepper, cored, seeded and thinly sliced
into rings
1 red pepper, cored, seeded and thinly sliced
into rings
4 medium trout
2 teaspoons red wine vinegar
7½ tablespoons plain unsweetened yogurt
2 hard-cooked eggs, finely chopped
salt
freshly ground black pepper

Preparation time: 20 minutes
Cooking time: 30 minutes

1. Melt half the margarine in a non-stick skillet and fry the onion and pepper rings over a moderate heat for 5 minutes, stirring often. Remove them with a slotted spoon and set aside to keep warm.

2. Melt the remaining margarine and fry the trout for 5-6 minutes on each side, until golden brown. Transfer the fish to a heated serving platter and keep warm.

3. Add the vinegar, yogurt and chopped egg to the pan, season with salt and pepper and stir well. Purée the sauce or press it through a sieve to make it smooth, then reheat it gently.

4. Return the fish and vegetable rings to the pan and heat through. Whole wheat bread and a green salad are good accompaniments to this summer dish.

MACKEREL WITH ORANGES

Serves 4

3 oranges
2 tablespoons soft margarine
2 scallions, finely chopped
2 tender celery stalks, finely chopped
3 oz cooked brown rice
1 teaspoon dried rosemary, crumbled
½ cup walnuts, chopped
salt
freshly ground black pepper
4 small mackerel, boned
1 small orange, peeled and cut into
thin slices, to serve

BAKED APPLE TROUT

Serves 4

4 medium trout
6 tablespoons dry cider
2 bay leaves
Filling:
1 tablespoon vegetable oil
1 small onion, peeled and finely chopped
3 oz whole wheat breadcrumbs
1 large cooking apple, peeled, cored and finely
chopped
1 teaspoon grated lemon rind
1 tablespoon lemon juice
1 tablespoon chopped parsley
1 teaspoon dried thyme
1 tablespoon sunflower seeds
3 tablespoons milk
salt
freshly ground black pepper

Preparation time: 25 minutes
Cooking time: 30 minutes
Oven: 350°F

1. Heat the oil in a small pan and fry the onion over moderate heat for 3 minutes, stirring once or twice.
2. Remove from the heat and stir in all the remaining filling ingredients. ☒
3. Spoon the filling into the cavities in the trout.
4. Place the fish head-to-tail in a greased, shallow baking dish, season with salt and pepper and pour over the cider. Add the bay leaves.
5. Bake the fish in a preheated oven for 25 minutes, basting with the cider from time to time. Serve with small potatoes boiled in their skins and a green vegetable.

☒ *Freeze the filling for up to 1 month. Thaw for 3 hours at room temperature or overnight in the refrigerator.*

Preparation time: 30 minutes
Cooking time: 45 minutes
Oven: 375°F

1. Grate the rind and squeeze the juice of 1 orange. Peel the second and chop the flesh. Thinly slice the third and reserve to garnish.
2. Melt the margarine in a small pan and fry the onion and celery over moderate heat for 3 minutes, stirring once or twice.
3. Remove from the heat and stir in the rice, rosemary, orange rind, chopped orange flesh, half the juice and the walnuts and season with salt and pepper.
4. Pack the filling into the fish and reshape.
5. Cut 4 pieces of foil about 12 × 7 inches and grease the center. Place a mackerel on each piece, make 3 diagonal slashes across the top, season with salt and pepper and sprinkle on the remaining orange juice. Close the foil, sealing the edges completely.
6. Place the foil parcels on a cookie sheet and bake for 40 minutes. Serve with the orange slices. Green salad with a sharp, lemony dressing is a good accompaniment.

From the left: Trout vinaigrette; Mackerel with oranges;
Baked apple trout.

COD AND CORN SOUFFLÉ

Serves 4

5 tablespoons fresh whole wheat breadcrumbs
12 oz cod fillet
1½ cups milk
1 bay leaf
4 tablespoons soft margarine
4 tablespoons whole wheat flour
3 tablespoons grated Parmesan cheese
1 cup frozen corn, thawed
4 tablespoons heavy cream
salt
freshly ground black pepper
3 egg yolks
4 egg whites, stiffly beaten
pinch of paprika

Preparation time: 30 minutes
Cooking time: 1 hour
Oven: 375°F

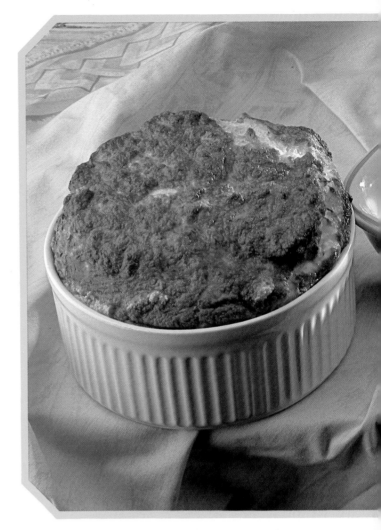

1. Grease a 2½ cup soufflé baker and sprinkle in the breadcrumbs to distribute them evenly.
2. Poach the fish in the milk with the bay leaf for 10 minutes. Drain the fish, reserving the liquor. Discard the bay leaf. Skin and flake the fish and remove any bones.
3. Melt the margarine in a small pan and stir in the flour. Pour in the fish liquor, stirring constantly until the sauce has thickened. Remove from the heat and leave to cool.
4. Stir in the cheese, corn and cream and season with salt and pepper. Beat in the egg yolks one at a time. Fold in the egg whites.
5. Pour the mixture into the prepared dish. Bake in a preheated oven for 40 minutes until the soufflé is well risen and golden brown. Serve at once, sprinkled with the paprika. Green salad makes a good balance of colour and texture.

From the left: Cod and corn soufflé; Baked herrings in ginger sauce; Ocean rolls.

OCEAN ROLLS

Serves 4

8 small flounder fillets, skinned
salt
freshly ground black pepper
1¼ tablespoons lemon juice
1¼ tablespoons chopped parsley, to garnish
lemon slices, to garnish
Filling:
1½ tablespoons soft margarine
4 bacon slices, rinded, chopped
1 cup mushrooms, finely chopped
1 cup fresh whole wheat breadcrumbs
1 cup frozen corn, thawed
1¼ tablespoons chopped parsley

Preparation time: 20 minutes
Cooking time: 30 minutes
Oven: 400°F

1. Melt the margarine and fry the bacon over moderate heat for 3-4 minutes. Stir in the mushrooms and cook for 2 minutes. Remove

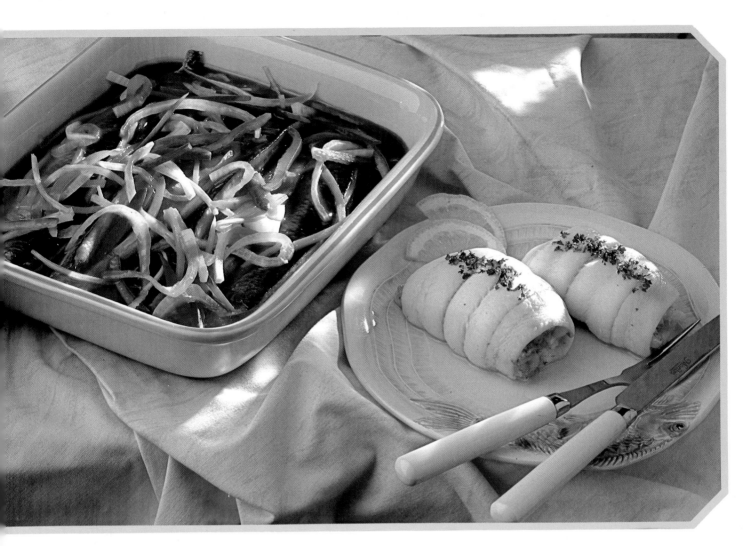

from the heat. Stir in the breadcrumbs, corn
and parsley and the salt and pepper.
2. Season the fillets with salt, pepper and lemon
   juice. Lay them skinned side up, divide the
   filling between them and roll up. Tie securely
   with fine twine.
3. Place the rolled fish in a greased, shallow
   baking dish. Cover with foil and bake in a
   preheated oven for 20 minutes. Remove strings
   and garnish with parsley and lemon slices.

BAKED HERRINGS IN GINGER SAUCE

Serves 4

4 herrings, boned
2 medium carrots, scraped, cut into matchstick
strips
2 celery stalks, cut into matchstick strips
1 red pepper, cored, seeded and thinly sliced
1 green pepper, cored, seeded and thinly sliced
1 large onion, peeled and thinly sliced

Sauce:
2 tablespoons red wine vinegar
1 tablespoon soy sauce
2 tablespoons dry sherry
2 tablespoons light honey
3 tablespoons water
1 teaspoon ground ginger
2 teaspoons cornstarch
freshly ground black pepper
pinch of cayenne pepper
1 inch piece ginger root, peeled and finely chopped

Preparation time: 15 minutes, plus marinating
Cooking time: 35-40 minutes
Oven: 375°F

1. Mix together the sauce ingredients.
2. Place the fish in a shallow baking dish, pour
   over the sauce, cover and leave for at least 2
   hours to marinate.
3. Turn the fish in the sauce. Add the carrots,
   celery, peppers and onion and cover with foil.
4. Bake in a preheated oven for 35-40 minutes and
   serve immediately.

SALMON STEAKS WITH ORANGE SAUCE

Preparation time: 10 minutes, plus marinating
Cooking time: 10 minutes

Serves 4

2½ tablespoons orange juice
4 salmon steaks, about 4 oz each
freshly ground black pepper
vegetable oil, for brushing
2 tablespoons butter, melted
asparagus tips, to serve
Sauce:
1 large egg
pinch of English mustard powder
salt
freshly ground black pepper
2½ teaspoons grated orange rind
1¼ tablespoons orange juice
½ cup sunflower oil

1. Sprinkle the orange juice over the salmon steaks, season with pepper and set aside at room temperature for at least 15 minutes.
2. Heat the broiler to high and brush the rack with oil. Brush the salmon steaks with half the melted butter and broil for 4 minutes. Turn the steaks, brush them with the remaining butter and broil for 5 minutes on the second side.
3. To make the sauce, put all the ingredients except the oil in a blender. Blend for 2-3 seconds. Then, with the machine running, pour in the oil gradually. Taste the sauce and adjust the seasoning if necessary.
4. Serve the fish with the sauce and asparagus.

Below: Salmon steaks with orange sauce.
Right: Grey mullet in mushroom sauce.

GREY MULLET IN MUSHROOM SAUCE

Serves 4

1 grey mullet, about 2¼ lb or 2, about 1¼ lb each, heads removed
4 tablespoons sunflower oil
Sauce:
1 large onion, peeled and thinly sliced
8 oz tomatoes, skinned and sliced
1½ cups mushrooms, sliced
½ cup chopped walnuts
1½ tablespoons chopped parsley
1 cup dry white wine
salt
freshly ground black pepper
coriander leaves or parsley, to garnish

Preparation time: 15 minutes
Cooking time: 45 minutes
Oven: 400°F

1. Cut 3 diagonal slashes in each side of the fish. Place the fish in a large ovenproof dish and broil under moderate heat for 5 minutes on each side. Cover the fish and keep warm.
2. Fry the onion for 3 minutes, then stir in the tomatoes and mushrooms, and cook for 5 minutes until softened.
3. Stir in the walnuts, parsley and wine, season with salt and pepper and bring to the boil. Simmer for 10 minutes.
4. Spoon the sauce over the fish and cook in a preheated oven for 15 minutes, until the fish is just firm.
5. Garnish with the coriander leaves or parsley.

NAVARRE SARDINES

Serves 4

1½ lb fresh sardines, heads removed
2 tablespoons milk
4 tablespoons whole wheat flour
1 teaspoon dried tarragon
pinch of cayenne pepper
sunflower oil, for brushing
sprigs of tarragon, to garnish
Sauce:
2 tablespoons sunflower oil
1 medium onion, peeled and finely chopped
1 celery stalk, finely chopped
1 red pepper, cored, seeded and finely chopped
2 tablespoons tomato paste
2 tablespoons red wine vinegar
1 tablespoon Worcestershire sauce
1 tablespoon soft dark brown sugar
1 teaspoon mustard
4 tablespoons orange juice
salt
freshly ground black pepper

Preparation time: 20 minutes
Cooking time: 40 minutes

1. To make the sauce, heat the oil and fry the onion, celery and pepper over moderate heat for 5 minutes, stirring often. Add the tomato paste, vinegar, Worcestershire sauce, sugar, mustard and orange juice, season with salt and pepper and bring to the boil. Simmer for 20 minutes, until the sauce thickens.
2. Brush the fish with milk and toss in flour seasoned with the tarragon and cayenne.
3. Heat the broiler to moderate. Brush the broiler pan with oil and broil the fish for 5-6 minutes, turning once.
4. Pour the sauce into a small bowl, stand it in the center of a heated serving dish and arrange the fish around it. Garnish with sprigs of tarragon.

CONFETTI COD

Serves 4

4 cod steaks, 5 oz each
4 teaspoons lemon juice
1¼ cups plain unsweetened yogurt
salt
freshly ground black pepper
½ teaspoon paprika
large pinch of cayenne pepper
½ cup frozen shrimp
1 cup small mushrooms, thinly sliced
unshelled shrimp, to garnish

Preparation time: 15 minutes
Cooking time: 20 minutes
Oven: 375°F

1. Sprinkle the fish with half the lemon juice.
2. Season the yogurt with salt, pepper, paprika, cayenne and the remaining lemon juice and stir in the shrimp.
3. Place each cod steak in the centre of a square of greased foil. Cover the fish with the mushrooms and pour on the shrimp sauce. Seal up the foil to make leakproof but loose parcels.
4. Place the fish parcels on a cookie sheet and cook in a preheated oven for 20 minutes.
5. To serve, slit open the parcels and garnish each one with unshelled shrimp. Rice is a good choice to serve with the fish.

From the left: Confetti cod; Navarre sardines; Baked fillets of sole.

BAKED FILLETS OF SOLE

Serves 4

4 small soles, 10 oz each
1 small onion, peeled and quartered
1 small carrot, scraped and halved lengthways
1 celery stalk, sliced
2 bay leaves
8 green peppercorns
1¼ tablespoons lemon juice
⅔ cup dry white wine
⅔ cup water
2 tablespoons butter
4 tablespoons flour
1¼ cups milk
4 tablespoons double cream
salt
freshly ground black pepper
pinch of ground coriander
2 kiwi fruits, peeled and sliced, to garnish

Preparation time: 40 minutes
Cooking time: 1 hour
Oven: 350°F

1. Skin and bone the sole, cutting each one into 4 fillets (or buy them ready filleted).
2. To make the stock, put the fish trimmings, onion, carrot, celery, bay leaves, peppercorns, lemon juice, wine and water into a pan. Bring to the boil, cover and simmer for 30 minutes, then strain.
3. Loosely roll the fish fillets, skinned side up, and place them in a shallow baking dish. Pour on the stock, cover with foil and bake in a preheated oven for 15 minutes.
4. Strain off the liquor and reserve. Keep the fish warm.
5. Melt the butter in a small pan, stir in the flour and pour on the milk and ⅔ cup of the fish liquor, stirring constantly. Bring to the boil, still stirring, and simmer for 3 minutes. Stir in the cream and season with salt, pepper and coriander.
6. Arrange the fish fillets on a heated serving dish, pour over the sauce and garnish with slices of kiwi fruit.

DEEP-DISH SEAFOOD PIE

Serves 4

1 lb haddock fillets
2 cups milk
1 bay leaf
6 black peppercorns
2 tablespoons butter
4 tablespoons flour
1 cup small mushrooms, sliced
¾ cup shelled shrimp
2 hard-cooked eggs, quartered
1½ tablespoons chopped parsley
1½ tablespoons capers
salt
freshly ground black pepper
pinch of cayenne pepper
Whole wheat pastry:
2 cups whole wheat flour
salt
½ cup soft margarine
⅔ cup rolled oats
cold water, to mix
1 egg, beaten, for brushing

Preparation time: 50 minutes, plus chilling pastry
Cooking time: 45 minutes
Oven: 400°F

1. To make the pastry, sift the flour and salt and mix in the margarine. Stir in the oats and use just enough cold water to form a dough. Knead the dough lightly. Wrap in plastic wrap or foil and chill for at least 30 minutes.
2. Poach the fish in the milk with the bay leaf and peppercorns for 10 minutes. Drain the fish, reserving the milk. Skin and flake the fish and remove any bones.
3. Melt the butter. Stir in the flour and gradually pour on the fish liquor, stirring constantly. Simmer the sauce for 3 minutes. Remove from the heat and cool a little.
4. Carefully stir the flaked fish, shrimp, mushrooms, eggs, parsley and capers into the sauce and season with salt, pepper and cayenne.
5. Turn the fish mixture into a 4½ cup pie pan.
6. Roll out the pastry on a lightly floured board. Cut off a strip and place it around the rim of the pan. Dampen the rim. Place the pastry on top, trim and flute the edges. Brush the pastry top with beaten egg.
7. Reroll the pastry trimmings and cut simple fish shapes. Place them in 'shoal formation' on the pie and brush with beaten egg. Make a slit in the center.
8. Bake the pie in a preheated oven for 25-30 minutes. Serve hot.

STIR-FRIED SHRIMP

Serves 4

½ lb broccoli flowerets, quartered
salt
4 tablespoons dry white wine
1¼ tablespoons cornstarch
1 egg white
2¼ cups shelled shrimp
5 tablespoons sunflower oil
2 scallions, thinly sliced
1 garlic clove, peeled and finely chopped
1 slice ginger root, peeled and finely chopped
3 medium zucchini, thinly sliced diagonally
Sauce:
4 tablespoons dry sherry
1¼ tablespoons tomato paste
1¼ teaspoons sugar
3 tablespoons soy sauce

Preparation time: 30 minutes
Cooking time: 10 minutes

Careful preparation is of great importance to the appearance of the dish. Slice the vegetables so that they are of even sizes. You can do this, and mix the sauce, in advance and store each ingredient in the refrigerator in separate lidded containers for up to 3-4 hours.

1. Mix together the sauce ingredients.
2. Blanch the broccoli in boiling, salted water for 1 minute. Drain, plunge at once into cold water, then drain again.
3. Stir the wine into the cornstarch to make a paste, then stir in the egg white. Pour this mixture over the shrimp.
4. Heat the oil in a large, heavy skillet or wok and stir-fry the scallions, garlic and ginger for 1 minute. Add the shrimp and stir-fry for 1 minute, then add the zucchini and continue stirring for 2 minutes.
5. Pour on the sauce, add the broccoli and stir for 2 minutes. Serve at once with rice.

From the top: Deep-dish seafood pie; Stir-fried shrimp.

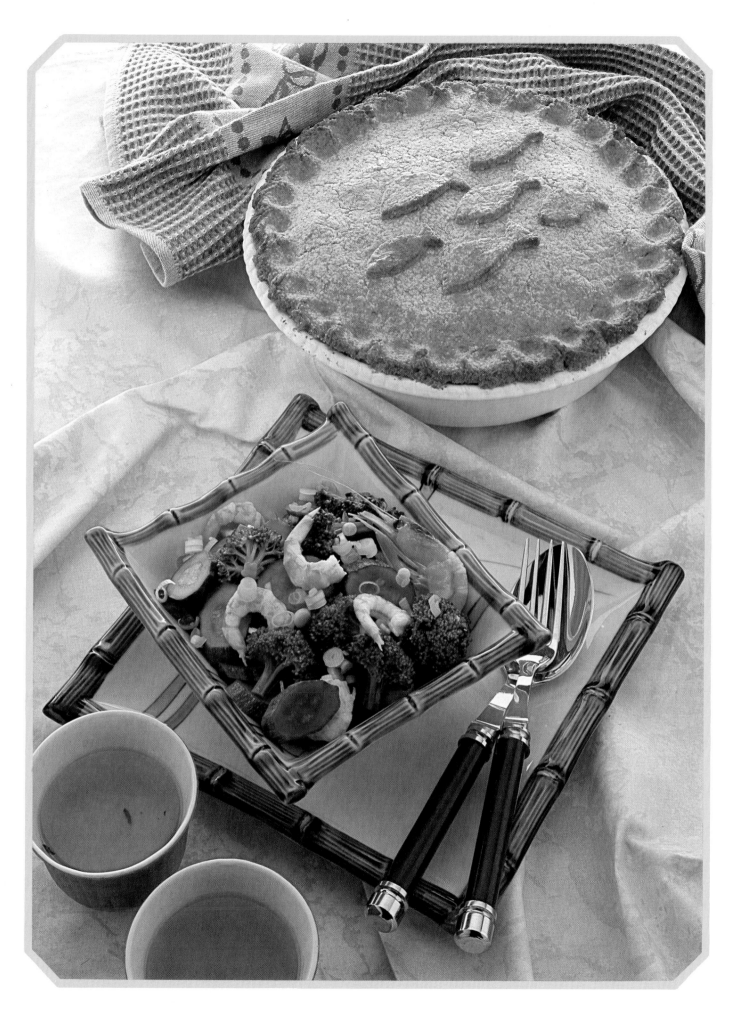

SHRIMP PATHIA

Serves 4

Preparation time: 15 minutes
Cooking time: 20 minutes

2½ tablespoons sunflower oil
1 medium onion, peeled and chopped
2 garlic cloves, peeled and finely chopped
1¼ teaspoons turmeric
¾ teaspoon chili powder
¾ teaspoon ground cumin
¾ teaspoon ground black pepper
½ teaspoon ground cardamom
pinch of ground cloves
1 teaspoon salt
1 bay leaf
⅔ cup tomato paste
3 cups shelled shrimp
⅔ cup boiling water
1¼ tablespoons lemon juice
2½ oz creamed coconut
1¼ teaspoons garam masala
2½ tablespoons chopped coriander leaves,
or parsley
unshelled shrimp, to garnish

1. Heat the oil in a large saucepan and fry the onion over moderate heat for 3 minutes, stirring once or twice. Add the garlic and fry for 1 minute. Stir in the turmeric, chili powder, cumin, pepper, cardamom, cloves, salt and bay leaf and cook for 1 minute. Stir in the tomato paste and the shrimp and cook for 2 minutes.
2. Pour on the water and lemon juice and bring to the boil. Stir in the creamed coconut and garam masala and simmer for 6-7 minutes until the sauce is thick.
3. Stir in half the chopped coriander. Sprinkle the remainder over the shrimp and garnish with unshelled shrimp. Rice is the traditional accompaniment to this Indian dish. A salad of thinly sliced raw zucchini tossed in plain unsweetened yogurt and mint is a cooling and refreshing contrast.

Below: Shrimp pathia.

TANDOORI FISH

Serves 4

1½ lb haddock fillets, skinned
lemon wedges, to garnish
Sauce:
1¼ cups plain unsweetened yogurt
2½ tablespoons lemon juice
1 small onion, peeled and finely chopped
1¼ tablespoons sweet paprika
¾ teaspoon cayenne pepper
1¼ teaspoons ground cumin
1¼ tablespoons tomato paste
salt
freshly ground black pepper
1 bay leaf

Preparation time: 10 minutes, plus 2 hours marinating
Cooking time: 15 minutes

If you use home made yogurt it is best to stabilize it before heating it, at stage 3. Stir it into 2⅓ teaspoons flour to make a paste then heat it slowly, stirring constantly.

1. Mix together all the sauce ingredients.
2. Place the fish in a shallow dish. Pour over half the sauce, cover and leave in the refrigerator to marinate for at least 2 hours. Refrigerate the reserved sauce.
3. Heat the broiler to moderate and line the pan with foil. Remove the fish and broil for 6 minutes on each side. Heat the sauce through gently in a small saucepan.
4. Garnish the fish with lemon wedges and serve the sauce separately. Serve with rice, broiled poppadoms and chutneys.

Above: Tandoori fish.

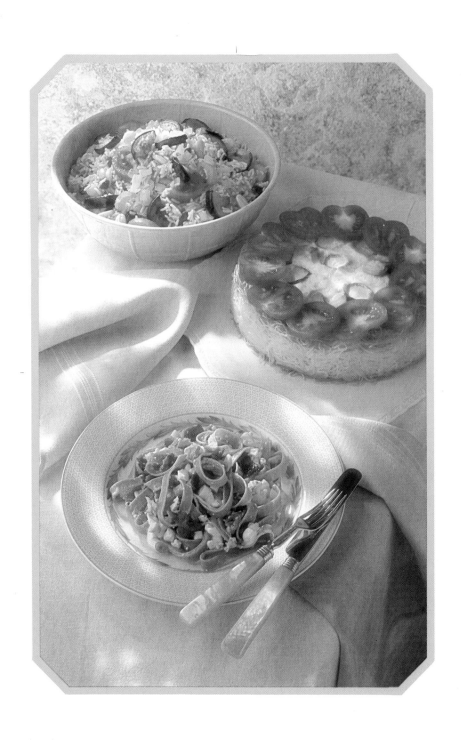

PASTA, PULSES & GRAINS

As a health food, pasta has only recently emerged due to the realisation that it isn't the pasta itself that makes us fat – it's the quantities of meat, cream and butter that we eat with it.

Choose whole wheat pasta and you have a product that retains the wheat germ and bran (ordinary pasta contains 0.3 per cent dietary fibre, whilst whole wheat kinds have a minimum of 10 per cent) and experiment with dressings and sauces made with low-fat cheeses, yogurt, crisp and lightly cooked vegetables and fresh herbs.

Dried peas and beans and grains (the seed of cereal plants) complement each other perfectly. While dried beans contain iron, B group vitamins and a high amount of proteins, they lack the amino acids of cereal foods. Thus a dish of black beans and rice (or indeed beans on whole wheat toast) comprises a full complement of protein.

Pre-soaking shortens the cooking time of beans and grains considerably. Soak dried beans overnight in cold water, or by the 'short' method: put them in cold water, bring to the boil, then soak for 1 hour. **Fast-boil all kidney beans for 15-20 minutes to dispel harmful toxins** and cook all pulses until they are only just tender.

BUCKWHEAT SPAGHETTI WITH SPICED CHICKEN

Serves 4

8 oz buckwheat spaghetti
salt
3½ tablespoons soft margarine
1 medium onion, peeled and finely chopped
1 garlic clove, peeled and finely chopped
1¼ teaspoons ground coriander
¾ teaspoon ground cardamom
2½ tablespoons whole wheat flour
⅔ cup plain unsweetened yogurt
2 cups chicken stock
1 cup diced cooked chicken
2 egg yolks
1½ tablespoons chopped fresh parsley
1 cup small mushrooms, thinly sliced
¾ cup fresh whole wheat breadcrumbs
3 tablespoons grated Parmesan cheese
sprig of parsley, to garnish

Preparation time: 20 minutes
Cooking time: 1 hour
Oven: 350°F

1. Cook the spaghetti in plenty of boiling, salted water for about 12 minutes, or according to the directions on the packet, until it is just tender. Drain, refresh in hot water, and drain again.
2. Melt the margarine and fry the onion over moderate heat for 3 minutes, stirring frequently. Add the garlic, coriander and cardamom and cook for 1 minute. Stir in the flour and cook for 1 minute. Remove the pan from the heat and gradually stir in the yogurt, then the stock. Simmer for 3 minutes. Remove from the heat and allow to cool a little.
3. Stir in the chicken, egg yolks and parsley.
4. Spread half the spaghetti in a greased, shallow baking dish and cover with half the chicken sauce. Arrange the mushrooms on top, then cover with the remaining spaghetti and then the sauce. Mix the breadcrumbs and cheese and sprinkle over the top.
5. Put the dish on a cookie sheet, place in a preheated oven and bake for 45 minutes. Serve hot, garnished with a sprig of parsley.

From the top: Mushroom and ham lasagne; Buckwheat spaghetti with spiced chicken.

MUSHROOM AND HAM LASAGNE

Serves 4-6

8 oz whole wheat lasagne
salt
2½ tablespoons olive oil
1 large onion, peeled and chopped
2 cups small mushrooms, thinly sliced
1¼ tablespoons flour
1¼ tablespoons lemon juice
1¼ cups plain unsweetened yogurt
freshly ground black pepper
¾ cup chopped walnuts
⅔ cup lean ham, cut into matchstick strips
1½ tablespoons chopped fresh parsley
Sauce:
1¼ cups plain unsweetened yogurt
1½ cups cheese, grated
7½ tablespoons whole wheat breadcrumbs

Preparation time: 40 minutes
Cooking time: 1 hour
Oven: 375°F

1. Cook the lasagne sheets in plenty of boiling, salted water for about 15 minutes, or according to the directions on the packet, until it is just tender, stirring occasionally. Drain, rinse in cold water and drain again. Pat the sheets dry with kitchen paper.
2. Heat the oil and fry the onion over moderate heat for 3 minutes, stirring frequently. Add the mushrooms and cook for 2 minutes. Stir in the flour and cook for 1 minute. Remove the pan from the heat and gradually stir in the lemon juice and yogurt. Cook, stirring, until the mixture thickens, then season. Simmer for 2 minutes. Stir in the walnuts, ham and parsley and remove from the heat.
3. Pour a layer of this sauce into a greased, shallow baking dish. Cover with sheets of lasagne and continue making layers, finishing with a layer of lasagne.
4. For the sauce, stir the yogurt and half the cheese together and pour over the dish. Sprinkle over the remaining cheese mixed with the breadcrumbs.
5. Stand the dish on a cookie sheet. Place in a preheated oven and bake for 25-30 minutes, or until the top is deep brown and the sauce bubbling.

CANNELLONI WITH SPINACH FILLING

Serves 4-6

1½ lb fresh spinach, stems removed
4 tablespoons butter
1 cup Ricotta or cottage cheese, sieved
½ cup grated Parmesan cheese
salt
freshly ground black pepper
pinch of grated nutmeg
2 large eggs
12 large cannelloni tubes
4 tablespoons flour
1¼ cups milk
5 tablespoons bran cereal

Preparation time: 50 minutes
Cooking time: 1 hour
Oven: 350°F

1. Wash the spinach and cook in the water clinging to the leaves in a large pan for 12 minutes over moderate heat. Stir frequently. Drain the spinach in a colander, pressing out all moisture. Chop the spinach finely.
2. Melt half the butter in a pan, add the spinach and stir well. Remove from the heat.
3. Beat the sieved cottage cheese and half the Parmesan cheese into the spinach and season with salt, pepper and nutmeg. Beat in the eggs. Set aside to cool.
4. Cook the cannelloni tubes in plenty of boiling, salted water for about 10 minutes, or according to the directions on the packet, until they are just tender. Drain, refresh in cold water, and drain again. Dry thoroughly with kitchen paper. Set aside to cool.
5. Melt the remaining butter in a pan, stir in the flour, and cook for 1 minute. Remove from the heat and gradually stir in the milk, stirring constantly. Bring to the boil, season with salt and pepper and simmer for 5 minutes. Taste and adjust the seasoning if necessary.
6. Use a pastry bag (but no tip) to fill the cannelloni tubes with the spinach mixture.
7. Place the filled cannelloni in a greased, shallow baking dish. Pour over the sauce and sprinkle with the remaining cheese mixed with the cereal.
8. Stand the dish on a cookie sheet. Place in a preheated oven and bake for 35-40 minutes, or until the topping is dark brown and crusty.

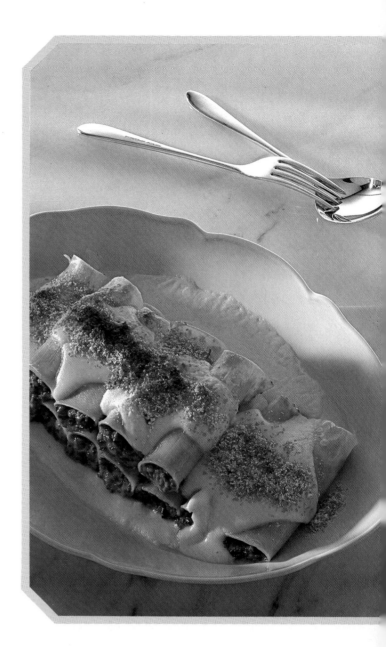

CARAMELLI WITH BASIL SAUCE

Serves 4

12 oz whole wheat pasta shells
salt
3 oz fresh basil leaves
5 tablespoons olive oil
3 garlic cloves, peeled and crushed
½ cup pine nuts, or blanched slivered almonds
⅓ cup grated Parmesan cheese
2 tablespoons softened butter
freshly ground black pepper

Preparation time: 15 minutes
Cooking time: 12 minutes

FLAMED TAGLIATELLE WITH YOGURT

Serves 4

12 oz whole wheat tagliatelle, or other
pasta shapes
salt
4 tablespoons butter
3 tablespoons brandy
⅔ cup plain unsweetened yogurt
½ cup grated Parmesan cheese
freshly ground black pepper
½ cup walnut halves, to garnish

Preparation time: 10 minutes
Cooking time: 10 minutes

1. Cook the tagliatelle in plenty of boiling, salted water for about 10 minutes, or according to the directions on the packet, until it is just tender. Drain, refresh in hot water, and drain again.
2. Melt the butter in a pan and toss the tagliatelle to coat thoroughly. Pour on the brandy, stir well and light it, to burn off the alcohol.
3. Stir in the yogurt and cheese, and season with plenty of black pepper. Garnish with the walnuts and serve at once.

This sauce, made with fresh basil leaves, is known as pesto, and originated in Genoa. You can grow basil during the summer in a greenhouse or on a sunny windowsill. However, if you do not have a plentiful supply, experiment with other herbs. Both marjoram and mint make interesting – though entirely different – substitutes.

1. Cook the pasta in plenty of boiling, salted water for about 12 minutes, or according to the directions on the packet, until it is just tender. Drain, refresh in hot water and drain again, tossing to ensure that no water is trapped inside. Keep hot.
2. To make the sauce, liquidize the herb leaves, oil, garlic and nuts in a blender. Scrape out the mixture, beat in the cheese and butter and season with pepper.
3. Spoon the sauce over the hot pasta and serve at once, as an accompaniment to meat and poultry, or on its own.

Clockwise from top right: Flamed tagliatelle with yoghurt; Caramelli with basil sauce; Cannelloni with spinach filling.

VERMICELLI PIE

Serves 4

½ lb vermicelli
salt
2 tablespoons butter
3-4 tablespoons olive oil
3 medium onions, peeled and chopped
3 medium zucchini, thinly sliced
1¼ teaspoons dried oregano
1¼ cups plain unsweetened yogurt
½ cup Gouda cheese, grated
2 eggs
freshly ground black pepper
2 large tomatoes, thinly sliced, to garnish

Preparation time: 25 minutes
Cooking time: about 1¼ hours
Oven: 350°F

1. Cook the vermicelli in plenty of boiling, salted water for about 12 minutes, or according to the directions given on the packet, until it is just tender. Drain, refresh in hot water, and then drain again. Return the vermicelli to the pan and toss with the butter over moderate heat until it is well coated.
2. Press the vermicelli into a greased 8 inch pie pan.
3. Heat 1½ tablespoons of the oil and fry the onions over moderate heat for 3 minutes, stirring frequently. Remove the onions with a draining spoon and set them aside.
4. Heat the remaining oil and fry the zucchini for 3-4 minutes, turning once, until they begin to soften. (If your skillet is not a non-stick one, you will need a little more oil.) Stir in the oregano and remove from the heat.
5. Scatter the onions over the base of the 'pie' case. Arrange the zucchini on top.
6. Beat the yogurt, cheese and eggs together and season with salt and pepper. Pour over the vegetables.
7. Place in a preheated oven and bake for 40-45 minutes, or until the filling is set. Serve hot, garnished with tomato rings.

MACARONI WITH PEPPER SAUCE

Serves 4

12 oz whole wheat macaroni
salt
5 tablespoons olive oil
1 large onion, peeled and sliced
3 garlic cloves, peeled and finely chopped
2 green peppers, cored, seeded and sliced into matchstick strips
1 yellow pepper, cored, seeded and sliced into matchstick strips
1 red pepper, cored, seeded and sliced into matchstick strips
12 oz tomatoes, peeled and sliced
2½ tablespoons chopped fresh parsley
black olives, to decorate
grated cheese, to serve (optional)

Preparation time: 30 minutes
Cooking time: 15 minutes

1. Cook the macaroni in plenty of boiling, salted water for about 12 minutes, or according to the directions on the packet, until it is just tender. Drain, refresh in hot water, and drain again. Keep hot.
2. Heat the oil and fry the onion, garlic and peppers over moderately high heat for about 5 minutes, or until they just begin to soften. Add the tomatoes, stir well and simmer for 10 minutes. Stir in half the parsley.
3. Turn the macaroni into a heated serving dish, pour on the sauce and toss well. Garnish with the black olives and the remaining parsley and serve with grated cheese in a separate dish.

From the left: Vermicelli pie; Macaroni with pepper sauce; Pasta twists with mussels.

PASTA TWISTS WITH MUSSELS

Serves 4

2 lb mussels
1¼ cups water
⅔ cup dry white wine
1 bunch dried herbs
12 oz whole wheat pasta twists
salt
4 tablespoons butter
freshly ground black pepper
1¼ cups plain unsweetened yogurt
2½ tablespoons chopped fresh parsley
fresh herbs, to garnish
grated Parmesan cheese, to serve

Preparation time: 1 hour
Cooking time: 30 minutes

1. Thoroughly wash the mussels in several bowls of clean water and pull off the beards. Tap the mussels and discard any that do not close. Put them in a large pan with the water and wine, bring to the boil, cover the pan and steam for 5-6 minutes, or until the shells have opened. Drain the mussels and reserve the cooking liquid. Discard any unopened mussels.
2. Pour the liquid into a pan, add the herbs, bring to the boil and fast-boil for 10 minutes, or until reduced by about two-thirds. Discard the herbs.
3. Cut the mussels away from the shells, leaving about 8 in the shells for garnish.
4. Cook the pasta in plenty of boiling, salted water for about 12 minutes, or according to the directions on the packet, until it is just tender. Drain, refresh in hot water, then drain again.
5. Melt the butter in the pan, add the pasta twists and mussels and season with pepper. Toss well. Beat the reserved shellfish liquid with the yogurt, stir in the parsley and pour over the pasta. Toss well.
6. Turn the pasta into a heated dish, garnish with fresh herbs and the reserved mussels in shells and serve with the Parmesan cheese.

EGGPLANT LAYER

Serves 4

1 medium eggplant, thinly sliced
salt
1⅔ cups whole wheat macaroni
5 tablespoons olive oil
12 oz ground lean beef
12 oz tomatoes, skinned and sliced
1¼ teaspoons dried oregano
1¼ tablespoons chopped fresh parsley
freshly ground black pepper
4 oz Feta cheese, very thinly sliced
1 cup small mushrooms, thinly sliced
1 cup fresh whole wheat breadcrumbs
⅓ cup grated Parmesan cheese

Preparation time: 30 minutes, plus draining
Cooking time: 1¼ hours
Oven: 350°F

1. Put the eggplant slices in a strainer over a dish and sprinkle with salt. Leave to drain for 30 minutes, then rinse thoroughly. Drain the slices and pat dry with kitchen paper.
2. Meanwhile, cook the macaroni in plenty of boiling salted water for about 12 minutes, or according to the directions on the packet, until it is just tender. Drain, refresh in hot water, and drain again.
3. Heat the oil in a pan and fry the eggplant slices, a few at a time, over moderate heat for 5 minutes for each batch. Remove from the pan as they are cooked and keep hot.
4. Fry the meat in the pan for 6 minutes, stirring frequently. Stir in the tomatoes and herbs and cook for 10 minutes. Season with salt and pepper.
5. In a greased, shallow baking dish make layers of the macaroni, eggplant, meat sauce, sliced cheese and mushrooms, finishing with the eggplant. Mix together the breadcrumbs and Parmesan cheese and sprinkle over the top. **F**
6. Put the dish on a cookie sheet. Place in a preheated oven and bake for 45 minutes. Serve hot with a green salad.

F *Freeze the uncooked dish for up to 2 months. Thaw in the refrigerator overnight, or bake from frozen for 1 hour.*

Clockwise from top left: Eggplant layer; Pasta twists with broccoli spears; Green noodles with blue cheese.

GREEN NOODLES WITH BLUE CHEESE

Serves 4

12 oz green spinach noodles, or other pasta shapes
salt
6 bacon slices, rinded and chopped
1 cup cottage cheese
½ cup blue cheese, crumbled
2 scallions, thinly sliced
freshly ground black pepper

Preparation time: 15 minutes
Cooking time: 15 minutes

1. Cook the noodles in plenty of boiling, salted water for 12 minutes, or according to the directions on the packet, until they are just tender. Drain, refresh in hot water, and drain again. Keep hot.
2. Fry the bacon over moderate heat until the fat has run and the bacon is crispy. Remove with a slotted spoon and reserve.
3. Toss the noodles with the cheeses and scallions and season with salt and pepper. Stir in the chopped bacon.
4. Turn the noodles into a heated serving dish. Serve at once.

PASTA TWISTS WITH BROCCOLI SPEARS

Serves 4

12 oz pasta twists, bows, or other shapes
salt
1 lb broccoli flowerets
1¼ tablespoons olive oil
1½ tablespoons butter
1 small onion, peeled and finely chopped
½ cup walnuts, roughly chopped
1½ oz anchovy, chopped
1½ tablespoons chopped fresh parsley
freshly ground black pepper
3 tablespoons grated Parmesan cheese

Preparation time: 20 minutes
Cooking time: 30 minutes

1. Cook the pasta in plenty of boiling salted water

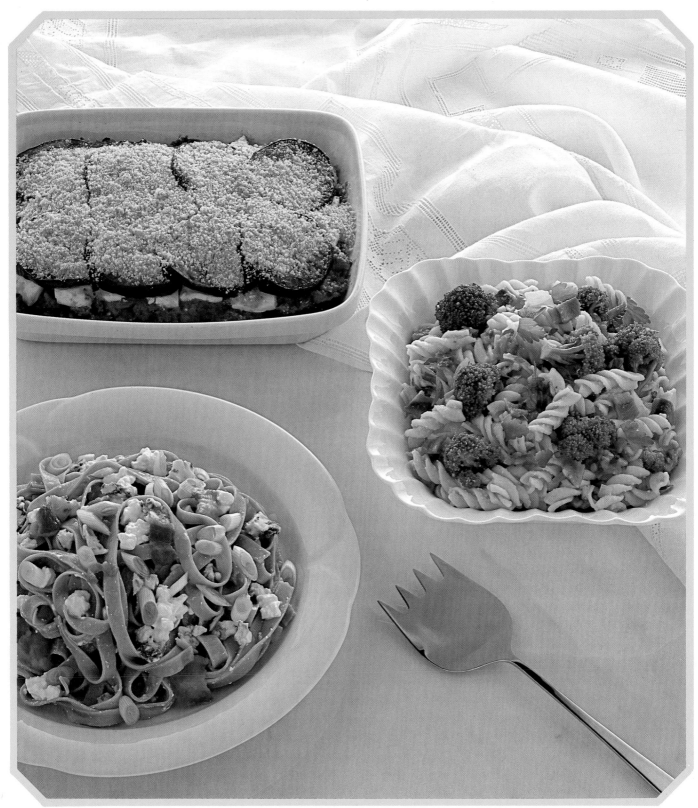

for 15 minutes, or according to the directions on the packet, until it is just tender. Drain immediately, refresh in hot water, and then drain once more.

2. Blanch the broccoli by cooking it in boiling salted water for 5 minutes. Drain, and plunge at once into cold water to prevent further cooking. Drain again.

3. Heat the oil with the butter and fry the onion over low heat for 10 minutes, stirring occa-·sionally.

4. Next, stir in the walnuts, anchovies and broccoli and cook slowly over gentle heat for 3-4 minutes.

5. Stir in the pasta and heat through. Remove from the heat, add the parsley, season well with pepper and stir in the cheese. Serve at once. A green salad makes a good accompaniment.

OLD-FASHIONED PEASE PUDDING

Serves 4

½ lb dried yellow split peas, soaked overnight and
drained
1 small onion, peeled and quartered
1 bunch of dried herbs
1¼ cups chicken stock (page 11)
1 large egg, lightly beaten
salt
freshly ground black pepper
1 teaspoon ground cumin
2½ tablespoons chopped fresh parsley
parsley sprigs, to garnish

Preparation time: overnight soaking, then 25 minutes
Cooking time: about 2¼ hours

1. Put the peas in a pan with the onion, herbs and chicken stock. Bring to the boil, cover and simmer for 1 hour, stirring occasionally, or until the peas are tender. Add a little more stock if the peas dry out before they are cooked. Discard the herbs.
2. Beat the peas to make a smooth purée, or purée them in a blender or food processor. Beat in the egg, season with salt, pepper and cumin and stir in the parsley.
3. Spoon the mixture into a greased 2½ cup mold and cover with foil. Stand on a trivet in a pan of boiling water. Cover the pan and steam for 1¼ hours.
4. Turn the pudding out on to a heated serving dish and garnish with the parsley sprigs.

From the left: Old-fashioned pease pudding; Mexican rice; Buckwheat spaghetti with almond sauce.

MEXICAN RICE

Serves 4

1¼ tablespoons sunflower oil
2 medium onions, peeled and sliced
1 red pepper, cored, seeded and chopped
1 cup brown rice
2½ cups chicken stock
8 small tomatoes, skinned and quartered
1 small avocado, pitted, peeled and cut into
½ inch chunks
4 eggs
4 tablespoons plain unsweetened yogurt
salt
freshly ground black pepper
2 tablespoons chopped coriander leaves, or finely
snipped chives, to garnish

Preparation time: 20 minutes
Cooking time: 1 hour

1. Heat the oil and fry the onion and pepper over moderate heat for 3 minutes, stirring frequently. Stir in the rice and cook for 1 minute. Stir in the stock and bring to the boil.
2. Cover the pan and simmer for 40 minutes.
3. Add the tomatoes and avocado, stirring in carefully to avoid breaking them up. Cover and simmer for 5 minutes.
4. Beat the eggs with the yogurt and season with salt and pepper. Pour over the rice and fork it over and over. Cook until the eggs are just set. Garnish with the coriander and serve at once.

BUCKWHEAT SPAGHETTI WITH ALMOND SAUCE

Serves 4

12 oz buckwheat spaghetti
salt
25 g (1 oz) butter
2½ tablespoons chopped fresh parsley
Sauce:
¾ cup ground almonds
¾ cup cottage cheese, sieved
⅓ cup grated Parmesan cheese
1¼ cups plain unsweetened yogurt
2½ tablespoons olive oil
pinch of grated nutmeg
pinch of ground cinnamon
freshly ground black pepper
10 tablespoons blanched almonds, toasted
1½ tablespoons chopped fresh parsley, to garnish

Preparation time: 20 minutes
Cooking time: about 12 minutes

1. Cook the spaghetti in plenty of boiling, salted water for about 12 minutes, or according to the directions on the packet, until it is just tender. Drain, refresh in hot water, and drain again. Return the spaghetti to the pan, toss it in the butter and parsley, cover and keep hot.
2. Mix all the sauce ingredients together except the toasted almonds and season with salt and pepper.
3. Turn the spaghetti into a heated serving dish. Stir the toasted almonds into the sauce, pour over the spaghetti and toss well. Garnish with chopped parsley and serve at once.

CORIANDER GARBANZO CASSEROLE

Serves 4

12 oz dried garbanzos, soaked overnight
and drained
1 small onion, peeled and quartered
a few parsley sprigs
2½ tablespoons sunflower oil
1 large onion, peeled and sliced
2 garlic cloves, peeled and finely chopped
4 celery stalks, thinly sliced
2 medium carrots, scraped and thinly sliced
1 red pepper, cored, seeded and thinly sliced
2½ teaspoons ground coriander
12 oz tomatoes, skinned and sliced
⅔ cup chicken stock
2½ tablespoons chopped fresh coriander leaves,
or parsley
salt
freshly ground black pepper

Preparation time: 25 minutes, plus soaking overnight
Cooking time: 4½ hours
Oven: 250°F

1. Put the garbanzos in a pan with the quartered onion and parsley, cover with water and bring to the boil. Cover and fast-boil for 5 minutes. Reduce the heat and simmer for 2 hours, or until the peas are tender. Drain the peas.

2. Heat the oil in a flameproof casserole and fry the sliced onion, garlic, celery, carrots, and red pepper over moderate heat for 4 minutes, stirring frequently. Stir in the ground coriander and cook for 1 minute.

3. Add the tomatoes, stock, peas, half the chopped herbs and season with salt and pepper. Bring to the boil and stir well.

4. Cover, place in a preheated oven and cook for 2 hours. Taste and adjust the seasoning if necessary. F Garnish with the remaining chopped herbs. Serve hot.

F *Cool the casserole and freeze it for up to 6 months. Thaw in the refrigerator overnight or at room temperature for 4-5 hours. You can also open-freeze the cooked and drained chick peas.*

KIDNEY BEAN AND CHICKEN PAELLA

Serves 6

5 tablespoons olive oil
1 large onion, peeled and finely chopped
2 garlic cloves, peeled and crushed
2 red peppers, cored, seeded and chopped
1½ cups brown rice
3¾ cups chicken stock
5 tablespoons dry sherry
1 teaspoon powdered saffron
2 chicken joints, skinned, boned and chopped
salt
freshly ground black pepper
8 oz red kidney beans, cooked
1 cup button mushrooms, sliced
1 cup frozen peas
6-8 unshelled shrimp, to garnish

Preparation time: 30 minutes
Cooking time: 1 hour

1. Heat the oil in a large skillet and fry the onion over moderate heat for 3 minutes, stirring frequently. Add the garlic, peppers and rice, stir well and cook for 1 minute.
2. Stir in the chicken stock and sherry, add the saffron and chicken and season with salt and pepper. Bring to the boil, cover and simmer for 30 minutes.
3. Stir in the beans, mushrooms and peas, cover and simmer for a further 15 minutes, or until the rice is tender and the stock has been absorbed completely.
4. Season with more black pepper and serve hot.

Left: Coriander garbanzo casserole.
Above: Kidney bean and chicken paella.

— 75 —

FELAFEL

Serves 4-6

½ lb dried soy beans, soaked overnight
and drained
1 large onion, peeled and grated
1 garlic clove, peeled and crushed
½ teaspoon ground coriander
½ teaspoon ground cumin
¼ teaspoon chili powder
a pinch of ground cloves
salt
freshly ground black pepper
1 tablespoon tahine (sesame seed paste)
2 teaspoons lemon juice
1 egg, lightly beaten
whole wheat flour, for coating
sunflower oil, for frying
1 lemon, quartered, to serve

Preparation time: 30 minutes, including overnight soaking
Cooking time: 2 hours

1. Cook the soy beans in boiling, unsalted water for 2 hours, or until they are tender. The actual time depends on the age and 'shelf-life' of the beans. Drain.
2. Grind the soy beans to a paste in a food processor, or pass them through a vegetable mill.
3. Beat in the onion, garlic, coriander, cumin, chili and ground cloves and season with salt and pepper. Beat in the tahine, lemon juice and enough of the egg to make a smooth paste.
4. Cover the paste and chill in the refrigerator for at least 30 minutes. This makes it much easier to handle.
5. Flour your hands, shape the mixture into rounds and press them into flat cakes. Dust all over with flour.
6. Heat very little oil and fry the cakes on both sides over moderate heat until brown. Serve hot, with the lemon wedges.

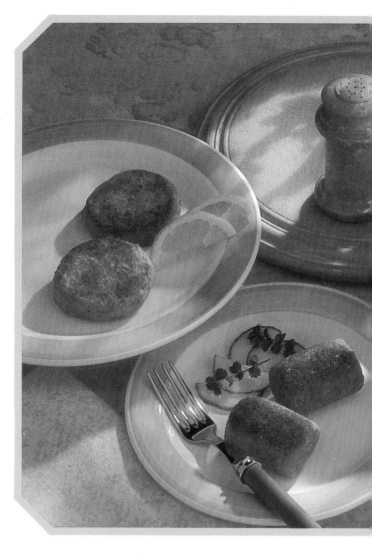

BULGAR CROQUETTES

Serves 4

2 medium carrots, scraped and quartered
salt
sunflower oil, for frying
2 medium onions, peeled and chopped
1 garlic clove, peeled and crushed
½ cup bulgar (cracked wheat)
6 tablespoons beef stock
2 tablespoons orange juice
2 tablespoons tomato paste
2 tablespoons chopped fresh parsley
1 teaspoon dried thyme
1 teaspoon orange rind
2 cups ground hazelnuts
freshly ground black pepper
wholewheat flour, to coat

Preparation time: 30 minutes
Cooking time: 40 minutes

OATY CAULIFLOWER AND BROCCOLI CHEESE

Serves 4

1 small cauliflower, divided into flowerets
½ lb broccoli flowerets
salt
1¼ cups plain unsweetened yogurt
1¼ tablespoons flour
⅓ cup cottage cheese
1½ cups Gouda cheese, grated
freshly ground black pepper
1 cup small mushrooms, sliced
2 tablespoons butter, melted
1 cup rolled oats
1 oz bran cereal
½ cup chopped hazelnuts

Preparation time: 25 minutes
Cooking time: 1 hour
Oven: 375°F

1. Cook the cauliflower and broccoli in boiling, salted water for 5 minutes. Drain and plunge them at once into cold water to retain colour and prevent further cooking. Drain again.
2. Stir a little of the yogurt into the flour to make a smooth paste, then stir in the remaining yogurt. Heat the yogurt mixture slowly, stirring constantly. Stir in the cottage cheese and half the grated cheese, season with salt and pepper and remove from the heat.
3. Put the mushrooms, cauliflower and broccoli into a greased, shallow baking dish, mix them carefully, pour on the cheese sauce and mix the vegetables to coat them thoroughly.
4. Stir the butter, oats, bran cereal and nuts together and stir in the remaining cheese. Sprinkle over the dish.
5. Place in a preheated oven and bake for 45 minutes. Serve hot.

1. Cook the carrots in boiling, salted water for 15 minutes, or until they are tender. Drain and chop finely.
2. Heat 4 tablespoons of the sunflower oil and fry the onion and garlic over moderate heat for 3 minutes, stirring frequently. Add the bulgar and carrot and cook, stirring, for 1-2 minutes. Add the stock, orange juice and tomato paste and stir well. Bring to the boil and simmer gently for 5 minutes.
3. Stir in the parsley, thyme, orange rind and hazelnuts and season with pepper.
4. Shape the mixture into 'sausages' and roll them in flour. F
5. Heat a very little oil in a skillet and fry the croquettes for 15 minutes over moderate heat, turning frequently to brown evenly all over. Serve hot.

F *Open-freeze the croquettes, then store them in a rigid container for up to one month. Thaw at room temperature for 2-3 hours.*

From the left: Felafel; Bulgar croquettes; Oaty cauliflower cheese.

NORTH OF THE BORDER PORRIDGE

Serves 4

5 cups boiling water
1⅓ cups medium oatmeal
about ½ teaspoon salt
To serve:
cold milk or buttermilk
light brown sugar or honey

Preparation time: 5 minutes
Cooking time: 25 minutes

1. Bring the water to the boil in a small pan.
   Sprinkle on the oatmeal, letting it trickle in a
   steady stream through your fingers, stirring all
   the time. Add the salt and stir until the mixture
   boils.
2. Simmer very gently for 20 minutes, stirring
   frequently to prevent lumps forming.
3. Serve at once with cold milk and sweetened
   with sugar or honey if liked.

DRIED FRUIT GRANOLA

Makes 2 lb

8 oz rolled oats
4 oz wheat flakes
2 oz wheatgerm
2 oz bran
2 oz sunflower seeds
1¼ cups mixed chopped nuts
½ cup dried apricots, chopped
¼ cup raisins
1 oz dried banana chips
¼ cup pitted dried dates, chopped

Preparation time: 20 minutes

1. Mix all the ingredients together. Store in an
   airtight container.
2. Serve the granola with plain unsweetened
   yogurt, buttermilk, skimmed or other milk or,
   for a delicious change, try it with unsweetened
   fruit juice.

SEED AND CEREAL GRANOLA

Makes 1 lb

6 oz rolled oats
2 oz wheat flakes
1½ oz stabilized wheatgerm
1½ oz bran
2 oz millet seeds
2 oz sesame seeds
1 oz pumpkin seeds

Preparation time: 5 minutes

1. Mix all the ingredients together and store in an airtight container.

FRESH VEGETABLE GRANOLA

Serves 2

1 small dessert apple, cored and thinly sliced
about 3 oz granola
1 small carrot, grated
1 celery stalk, thinly sliced
2½ tablespoons small cauliflower flowerets
2½ teaspoons lemon juice
1¼ tablespoons chopped hazelnuts
2½ tablespoons raisins

Preparation time: 10 minutes

1. Toss the apple slices in the lemon juice to prevent discoloration.
2. Mix all the ingredients together. Serve with buttermilk and top with plain unsweetened yogurt.

From the left: North of the border porridge; Dried fruit granola; Seed and cereal granola; Fresh vegetable granola.

EGGPLANT PILAFF

Serves 4-6

1½ tablespoons butter
6½ tablespoons olive oil
1 large onion, peeled and finely chopped
2 celery stalks, thinly sliced
1 garlic clove, peeled and crushed
1⅓ cups brown rice, washed and drained
3¾ cups chicken stock
1 teaspoon dried thyme
salt
freshly ground black pepper
1 medium eggplant, sliced, then quartered
2 large tomatoes, skinned and sliced
¼ cup blanched almonds
¼ cup raisins

Preparation time: 25 minutes
Cooking time: 1 hour
Oven: 350°F

1. Melt the butter with 1½ tablespoons of the oil in a flameproof casserole and fry the onion and celery over moderate heat for 3 minutes, stirring frequently. Add the garlic and rice, stir well and cook for 1 minute.
2. Stir in the stock, add the thyme and season with salt and pepper. Bring to the boil and stir thoroughly.
3. Cover the casserole, place in a preheated oven and cook for 45 minutes, or until the rice is tender and the stock has been absorbed.
4. While the rice is cooking, heat the remaining oil in a pan and fry the eggplant and tomatoes over moderate heat for 6-7 minutes, stirring frequently, or until they are tender. Season with black pepper.
5. Stir the eggplant, tomatoes, almonds and raisins into the rice. Cover and return to the oven for 5 minutes. Serve hot.

CHICKEN AND WHOLE WHEAT RISOTTO

Serves 4

½ lb whole wheat grains
salt
2 tablespoons butter
2½ tablespoons olive oil
1 large onion, peeled and thinly sliced
2 garlic cloves, peeled and finely chopped
1 chicken breast, skinned, boned and diced
2 cups mushrooms, thinly sliced
2 green peppers, cored and thinly sliced
1¼ cups chicken stock
2½ tablespoons medium sherry
1 teaspoon dried oregano
freshly ground black pepper
few sprigs fresh parsley
2½ tablespoons walnut halves
grated Parmesan cheese, to serve

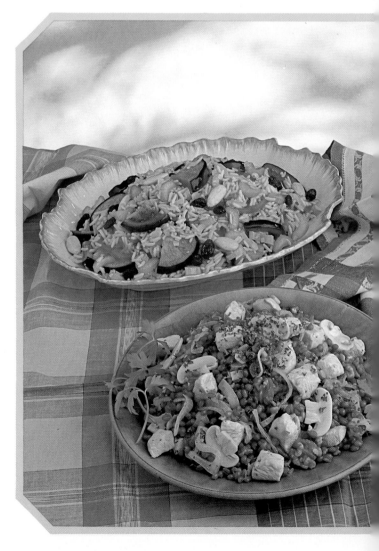

Preparation time: 20 minutes
Cooking time: 1 hour 40 minutes

1. Partly cook the wheat grains in a large pan of boiling, salted water for 1 hour. Drain.
2. Melt the butter with the oil in a large skillet and fry the onion and garlic over moderate heat for 3 minutes, stirring frequently. Add the partly-cooked wheat, stir well and cook for 1 minute. Stir in the chicken, mushrooms and peppers and cook for 2 minutes.
3. Stir in the stock and sherry, add the oregano and season with salt and pepper.
4. Bring to the boil, cover the pan and simmer for 30 minutes, or until the wheat is tender and the stock has been absorbed.
5. Finely chop 2-3 sprigs parsley. Stir in with the walnuts and serve at once with more sprigs of parsley. Serve the cheese separately.

From the left: Eggplant pilaff; Chicken and whole wheat risotto; Rice and bean salad.

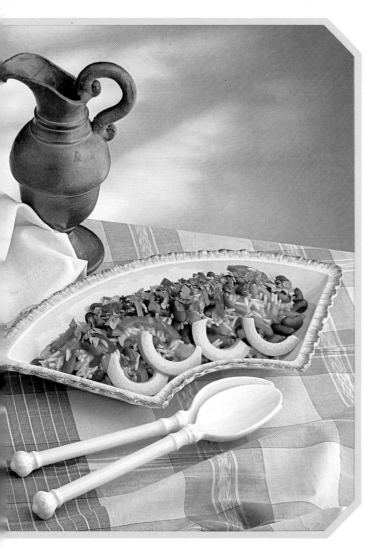

RICE AND BEAN SALAD

Serves 4-6

8 oz black beans, soaked overnight and drained
2½ tablespoons sunflower oil
1 medium onion, peeled and chopped
1 garlic clove, peeled and crushed
1 green pepper, cored, seeded and thinly sliced
1 red pepper, cored, seeded and thinly sliced
2 red chilis, cored, seeded and finely chopped
(optional)
4 large tomatoes, skinned and sliced
salt
freshly ground black pepper
½-1 teaspoon chili powder (or to taste)
1 cup long-grain brown rice
1¼ cups chicken stock
To garnish:
1¼ tablespoons chopped fresh coriander leaves, or
fresh parsley sprigs
1 avocado, seeded, peeled and sliced
1 tablespoon lemon juice

Preparation time: 30 minutes, plus soaking overnight
Cooking time: 2 hours

1. Cook the beans in fast boiling, unsalted water for 15 minutes. Reduce the heat and simmer for a further 45 minutes or until they are almost tender. Drain.
2. Heat the oil and fry the onion over moderate heat for 3 minutes, stirring frequently. Add the garlic, peppers and chilis, stir well and cook for 2 minutes.
3. Add the tomatoes, salt, pepper and chili powder and cook for 1 minute. Add the rice, stock and beans and bring to the boil.
4. Cover the pan and simmer for 45 minutes, or until the rice is tender and the stock has been absorbed completely.
5. Garnish with the coriander leaves and the avocado slices tossed in lemon juice.

MILLET AND FAVA BEAN PILAFF

Serves 4-6

8 oz millet seeds
2½ cups chicken stock
salt
1 lb dried fava beans
2½ tablespoons sunflower oil
1 large onion, peeled and sliced
½ lb zucchini, thinly sliced
1 green pepper, cored, seeded and chopped
2 cardamom pods, peeled and seeds
lightly crushed
1½ teaspoons cumin seeds
freshly ground black pepper
2 large tomatoes, skinned and sliced
5 tablespoons golden raisins
parsley sprigs to garnish

Preparation time: 25 minutes
Cooking time: 25 minutes

1. Put the millet in a saucepan with the chicken stock and add a little salt. Bring to the boil, stir thoroughly, then cover the pan and simmer for 20 minutes, stirring occasionally, or until the millet is tender and all the stock has been absorbed.

2. Cook the fava beans in boiling, salted water until they are tender. Drain.

3. Heat the oil and fry the onion, zucchini and green pepper over moderate heat for 4-5 minutes, stirring frequently. Stir in the crushed cardamom seeds and cumin seeds, then season with salt and pepper and cook for 1 minute. Add the tomatoes, stir in well and simmer for 3 minutes.

4. Stir the fava beans and millet into the vegetables, stir in the golden raisins and heat gently. Garnish with the parsley sprigs and serve hot.

VEGETABLE FRIED RICE

Serves 4

2 large eggs
1¼ tablespoons water
freshly ground black pepper
1½ tablespoons butter
2½ tablespoons sunflower oil
3 medium leeks, thinly sliced
2 cups small mushrooms, thinly sliced
¾ cup cashew nuts
1 cup frozen peas, defrosted
2½ tablespoons soy sauce
½ lb cooked brown rice, cold
2½ tablespoons chopped fresh mint

Preparation time: 20 minutes
Cooking time: 25 minutes

1. Beat the eggs with the water and season with pepper. Melt the butter in an omelette pan and, when it is hot, pour in the egg mixture. Tip the pan to spread the mixture evenly and cook over moderate heat until it is set on one side. Flip the omelette over and cook it to brown the other side. Tip it on to a plate and leave it to cool.
2. Heat the oil in a pan and fry the leeks over moderate heat for 3 minutes, stirring frequently. Add the mushrooms, nuts and peas and stir well. Cook for 1 minute. Stir in the soy sauce and rice and season with pepper. Cook for 5 minutes, stirring frequently.
3. Cut the omelette into thin strips.
4. Stir the mint into the rice and adjust the seasoning if necessary.
5. Turn the rice into a heated serving dish and garnish with the omelette strips arranged in a lattice pattern. Serve hot.

GREEN RICE

Serves 4

1 cup brown rice
salt
2½ cups chicken stock
4 celery stalks, finely sliced
5 tablespoons chopped celery leaves
½ lb spinach, trimmed and finely chopped
5 tablespoons chopped fresh parsley
freshly ground black pepper
2 tablespoons butter
To garnish:
watercress sprigs

Preparation time: 30 minutes
Cooking time: 50 minutes

1. Put the rice, salt and stock into a pan, stir well and bring to the boil. Cover and simmer gently for 40 minutes.
2. Stir in the sliced celery, the celery leaves, spinach and parsley and season with pepper. Cover the pan and simmer for 5 minutes. Stir in the butter.
3. Turn the rice into a heated serving dish and garnish it with the watercress.

From the left: Millet and fava bean pilaff; Vegetable fried rice; Green rice.

GNOCCHI WITH TOMATO SAUCE

Serves 4-6

4½ cups milk
salt
1 cup whole wheat semolina
⅔ cup grated Parmesan cheese
2 tablespoons butter
2 egg yolks
½ teaspoon grated nutmeg
freshly ground black pepper
1¼ tablespoons chopped fresh oregano,
or parsley, to garnish
Sauce:
1 lb tomatoes, skinned and chopped
1¼ tablespoons lemon juice
2½ tablespoons tomato paste
1 teaspoon light brown sugar
⅔ cup sweet cider
1¼ teaspoons dried oregano

Preparation time: 30 minutes
Cooking time: 45 minutes
Oven: 450°F

1. Boil the milk, add salt and gradually stir in the semolina. Simmer very gently for 15 minutes, stirring frequently, until the mixture thickens.
2. Remove from the heat and beat in half the cheese, the butter and the egg yolks.
3. Spread the mixture over a dampened cookie sheet to a depth of ½ inch and level the top. Leave for at least 1 hour to cool completely.
4. With a 2½ inch cookie cutter, cut out rounds of the paste and lift them up with a spatula. Arrange them in overlapping circles in a greased, shallow baking dish.
5. Sprinkle the remaining cheese over the dish and sprinkle with the nutmeg.
6. Place in a preheated oven and bake for 20 minutes.
7. To make the sauce, put all the ingredients in a small pan, season well with salt and pepper and bring to the boil. Simmer for 20 minutes, or until the sauce thickens. Beat it thoroughly, taste and adjust the seasoning.
8. Serve the gnocchi garnished with the oregano or parsley, and the sauce separately.

SPICY DHAL

Serves 4

½ lb yellow split peas, soaked overnight
and drained
2½ tablespoons sunflower oil
1 large onion, peeled and chopped
2 garlic cloves, peeled and finely chopped
2½ teaspoons ground cumin
1¼ teaspoons ground turmeric
2 scallions, thinly sliced
2½ teaspoons lemon juice
salt
freshly ground black pepper
1½ tablespoons chopped fresh coriander leaves,
or parsley
To garnish:
a few coriander leaves or parsley sprigs
small scallions

Preparation time: 20 minutes, plus overnight soaking
Cooking time: 50 minutes

1. Cook the split peas in boiling, unsalted water for 30-40 minutes, or until they are tender. Drain thoroughly.
2. Heat the oil and fry the onion and garlic over moderate heat for 3 minutes, stirring frequently. Stir in the cumin and turmeric and cook for 3 minutes.
3. Stir in the split peas, scallions and lemon juice and season with salt and pepper. Cook for a further 2-3 minutes, then taste and adjust the seasoning if necessary. **F**
4. Turn the mixture into a heated serving dish, sprinkle over the chopped coriander and garnish with scallions. Serve hot.

F *Freeze for up to 2 months. Thaw at room temperature for 3-4 hours then gently reheat on top of the cooker.*

From the top: Gnocchi with tomato sauce; Spicy dhal.

VEGETABLES & SALADS

Colorful roots, crisp leafy greens, succulent pods and seeds, flavor-absorbing squashes – vegetables are far too delicious and nutritious to be relegated to the supporting role for they offer an endless and tempting variety as main dishes.

Sadly, all forms of cooking rob vegetables of some of their nutrients and vitamins – especially vitamin C – which disperse in water, heat and on exposure to the air, not only in cooking, but in storage and soaking too. Rinse vegetables quickly in water and scrub rather than peel when possible. Potato skins, for example, can be quickly rubbed off after cooking. Steam or simmer in the minimum of water, or bake until only just tender.

Salads must surely be the most nutritious of all fast foods. Choose only the freshest and youngest ingredients and prepare and serve them as soon as possible with the lightest of dressings.

To retain the maximum crispness, toss salad greens in the dressing just before serving. Raw cabbage, celery, mushrooms and peppers may benefit – it's a matter of choice – from being marinated in the dressing for a half-hour or so, and cooked dried beans absorb more flavor if they are coated while still hot in an aromatic dressing.

VEGETABLE MOUSSAKA

Serves 4

4 oz brown lentils, soaked overnight and drained
1 lb tomatoes, skinned and chopped
1 bay leaf
1¼ teaspoons dried oregano
1¼ teaspoons dark brown sugar
salt
freshly ground black pepper
sunflower oil, for frying
1 large eggplant, thinly sliced
1 lb potatoes, peeled and thinly sliced
Sauce:
2 tablespoons soft margarine
4 tablespoons whole wheat flour
1¼ cups milk
⅔ cup plain unsweetened yogurt
1 cup Feta cheese, crumbled
1 egg
large pinch of grated nutmeg

Preparation time: 30 minutes, plus overnight soaking
Cooking time: 2 hours
Oven: 375°F

1. Cook the lentils in boiling, unsalted water for 1 hour. Drain.
2. Simmer the tomatoes with the bay leaf, oregano, sugar, salt and pepper for 20 minutes.
3. Stir the lentils into the tomato mixture and simmer for 10 minutes, stirring, until thick.
4. Heat the oil and fry the eggplant slices a few at a time over moderate heat until they begin to colour.
5. Cook the potato slices in boiling, salted water for 10 minutes, or until they begin to soften.
6. Make layers of the tomato and lentil sauce, eggplant and potatoes in a greased casserole, finishing with potatoes.
7. Melt the margarine and stir in the flour. Cook for 1 minute, then remove the pan from the heat. Gradually stir in the milk, then the yogurt. Bring to the boil then simmer for 3 minutes. Remove from the heat. Beat in half of the cheese, and the egg and season with salt, pepper and nutmeg.
8. Pour the sauce over the dish and sprinkle the remaining cheese on top.
9. Stand the casserole on a cookie sheet. Place in a preheated oven and bake for 35-40 minutes, or until the sauce is bubbling and browned.

ASPARAGUS QUICHE

Serves 6

1½ cups whole wheat self-rising flour
salt
4 tablespoons vegetable shortening
2 tablespoons butter
3 tablespoons cottage cheese, strained
1 teaspoon fennel seeds, lightly crushed
cold water, to mix
Filling:
¾ lb asparagus, cooked and drained
6 tablespoons curd cheese
⅔ cup plain unsweetened yogurt
7½ tablespoons milk
2 eggs
freshly ground black pepper

Preparation time: 25 minutes, plus chilling
Cooking time: 1 hour
Oven: 375°F

1. Sift the flour and salt together and tip the bran from the sieve back into the bowl. Rub in the fats until the mixture is like fine breadcrumbs. Stir in the cheese and fennel and mix to a dough with a very little water. Knead the dough lightly. Wrap in foil and chill for at least 30 minutes.

2. Roll out the pastry on a lightly floured board and use to line a greased 8 inch pie pan.

3. Arrange the asparagus in a wheel pattern in the pie pan.

4. Mix the cheese, yogurt and milk together, beat in the eggs and season with salt and pepper. Pour the filling into the pastry case.

5. Place in a preheated oven and bake for 40-45 minutes, until the filling is set. F Serve warm.

F *Freeze for up to 2 months. Reheat from frozen in the oven for about 30 minutes.*

Clockwise from the left: Vegetable moussaka; Fruity eggplant boats; Asparagus quiche.

FRUITY EGGPLANT BOATS

Serves 4

4 eggplants, about 6 oz each
salt
6½ tablespoons sunflower oil
1 large onion, peeled and chopped
2 garlic cloves, peeled and finely chopped
1 lb tomatoes, skinned and sliced
6 tablespoons golden raisins
¼ cup raisins
¾ cup blanched, slivered almonds
2½ tablespoons chopped fresh parsley
1 teaspoon dried thyme
freshly ground black pepper
parsley, to garnish

Preparation time: 25 minutes
Cooking time: 1¼ hours
Oven: 350°F

1. Cut off the stalk ends of the eggplants and halve them lengthways. Scoop out the flesh (a curved grapefruit knife is ideal for this), leaving firm 'walls'. Chop the eggplant flesh finely and put it in a strainer. Sprinkle liberally with salt and leave for about 1 hour, to degorge (draw off the bitter juices).

2. Rinse the eggplant in cold water and drain thoroughly on kitchen paper.

3. Heat the oil and fry the onion, garlic and eggplant over a moderate heat for 5 minutes, stirring frequently.

4. Add the tomatoes, stir well and fry for a further 5 minutes.

5. Stir in the golden raisins, raisins, almonds, parsley and thyme and season with salt and pepper.

6. Stand the eggplant shells cut side up in a greased baking pan and fill them with the tomato mixture.

7. Place in a preheated oven and bake the eggplants for 1 hour. Serve hot, garnished with the parsley leaves.

CABBAGE BASKET

Serves 4

1 small white or green cabbage
salt
1 lb carrots
4 tablespoons soft margarine
1 medium onion, peeled and chopped
1 garlic clove, peeled and crushed
1¼ teaspoons ground ginger
1¼ tablespoons clear honey
4 oz cooked brown rice
½ cup hazelnuts, chopped
freshly ground black pepper
¾ cup fresh whole wheat breadcrumbs
1 hard-cooked egg, finely chopped
1½ tablespoons chopped fresh parsley

Preparation time: 1 hour
Cooking time: 1¾ hours

1. Remove any damaged or discolored outer leaves from the cabbage and trim to a neat shape. Blanch in boiling, salted water for 5 minutes. Drain thoroughly.
2. Cook the carrots in boiling, salted water for 10 minutes. Drain, reserving the liquid, and chop them finely.
3. Place the cabbage on a board. With 2 large spoons, gently pull a few leaves outwards, to expose the centre leaves and stalk. Remove these, leaving firm 'walls' about 1 inch thick. Finely chop the centre leaves.
4. Melt half the margarine and fry the onion and garlic over moderate heat for 3 minutes, stirring once or twice. Stir in the chopped cabbage, carrots, ginger, honey, rice, half the hazelnuts and 5 tablespoons of the reserved carrot stock. Season with salt and pepper, remove from the heat and stir well.
5. Pack the filling into the cabbage 'basket' and wrap it lightly in foil.
6. Stand the cabbage on a trivet in a pan of fast-boiling water, reduce the heat, cover the pan and cook for 1½ hours.
7. Melt the remaining margarine and fry the breadcrumbs and reserved nuts. Stir in the egg and parsley.
8. Transfer the cabbage to a heated serving platter and sprinkle the crumb mixture on top. Serve hot, cut into wedges.

Clockwise from the left: Cabbage basket; Kitchen-garden loaf; Celery and walnut roll.

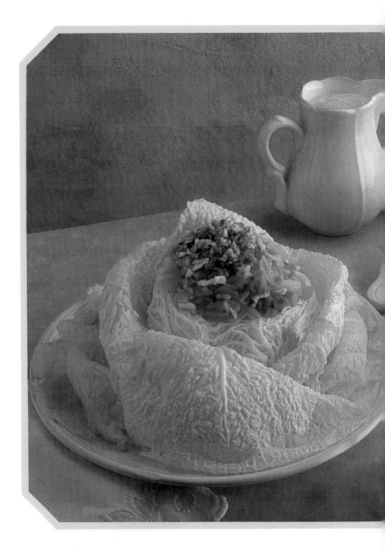

KITCHEN-GARDEN LOAF

Serves 6-8

2 medium carrots, scraped and cut into matchstick strips
6 oz asparagus
6 oz snap beans
salt
2 tablespoons soft margarine
1 medium onion, peeled and chopped
1 garlic clove, peeled and crushed
2 cups small mushrooms, chopped (reserve 2 for garnish)
1 cup cottage cheese
½ cup blue cheese, crumbled
4 eggs
⅔ cup plain unsweetened yogurt
1½ tablespoons chopped fresh parsley
1 teaspoon dried thyme
½ teaspoon grated nutmeg
freshly ground black pepper
1 hard-cooked egg, sliced, to garnish

them lengthways along the tin. Pour in one third of the remaining mixture and top with a layer of carrots. Pour on one-half of the remaining mixture, top with a layer of beans then pour on the rest of the egg.

6. Stand in a roasting tin half filled with water. Cover with foil. Place in a preheated oven and bake for 1½ hours, or until the egg custard is set. Cool the tin on a wire rack, then chill.

7. Turn the loaf out on to a plate. Garnish with slices of egg and the reserved mushrooms. Leave at room temperature for 30 minutes.

8. To make the dressing, mix all the ingredients together and serve chilled.

CELERY AND WALNUT ROLL

Serves 4

4 eggs, separated
¾ cup Gruyère cheese, grated
2 teaspoons celery seed
4 tablespoons celery leaves, finely chopped
Filling:
¾ cup curd cheese
¾ cup walnuts, chopped
2 tablespoons chopped parsley
freshly ground black pepper
celery leaves, to garnish

Preparation time: 25 minutes
Cooking time: 30 minutes
Oven: 400°F

1. Line a jelly roll pan with greased waxed paper.
2. Beat the egg yolks until they are creamy, then beat in one-third of the cheese, celery seed and celery leaves.
3. Whisk the egg whites until stiff and fold them into the celery mixture. Spread the mixture over the prepared tin and level the top.
4. Place in a preheated oven and bake for 25 minutes, or until firm to the touch.
5. Beat together the curd cheese, walnuts and parsley and season with pepper.
6. Remove the tin from the oven. Spread the filling over the sponge base and, using the paper to lift it up, roll it up from one short end.
7. Lift the roll on to a heatproof dish. Sprinkle the remaining cheese on top and return it to the oven for 3-4 minutes to melt the cheese. Serve hot, garnished with celery leaves.

Dressing:
⅔ cup plain unsweetened yogurt
1 teaspoon French mustard
½ teaspoon curry powder
2 tablespoons heavy cream
1 teaspoon lemon juice

Preparation time: 45 minutes
Cooking time: 1¾ hours
Oven: 350°F

1. Cook the carrots, asparagus and beans in boiling, salted water until they are just tender. Drain and plunge at once into cold water to prevent further cooking. Drain again. Pat dry.
2. Grease a 5 cup bread pan and line it with greased waxed paper.
3. Melt the margarine and gently fry the onion and garlic for 3 minutes, stirring. Add the mushrooms and cook for 3 minutes.
4. Blend the onion mixture with the cheese, eggs, yogurt and parsley until smooth. Add the thyme and nutmeg and season.
5. Pour one quarter of the egg and cheese mixture into the prepared pan. Lay the asparagus over

SOUFFLÉ ZUCCHINI

Serves 4

6 medium zucchini
salt
12 oz tomatoes, skinned and sliced
1¼ teaspoons dried oregano
freshly ground black pepper
1¼ tablespoons tomato paste
1¼ teaspoons lemon juice
2 eggs, separated
1 egg white
¾ cup Gruyère cheese, grated
pinch of cayenne pepper

Preparation time: 20 minutes
Cooking time: 1 hour
Oven: 350°F

1. Cook the zucchini in boiling, salted water for 5 minutes. Drain and cut off the ends. Slice the zucchini in half lengthways and scoop out the flesh, leaving firm 'walls'. Chop the flesh. Leave to cool.
2. Put the tomatoes, oregano, pepper, tomato paste and lemon juice into a pan, stir well and bring to the boil.
3. Beat the egg yolks and chopped zucchini flesh together. Whisk the egg whites and fold into the egg yolk mixture with ½ cup of the cheese, salt, pepper and cayenne.
4. Spoon the tomato sauce into a baking pan. Arrange the zucchini halves on top, cut sides up, and spoon the soufflé mixture into the 'shells'. Sprinkle over the remaining cheese.
5. Place in a preheated oven and bake the zucchini for 35 minutes, or until the cheese mixture is well risen and firm. Serve at once.

Above: Soufflé zucchini.
Right: Vegetable cobbler.

VEGETABLE COBBLER

Serves 6

3 medium carrots, scraped and thinly sliced
½ small cauliflower, divided into florets
salt
¼ cup soft margarine
8 small leeks, thickly sliced
2 small heads fennel, sliced
¼ cup whole wheat flour
2 cups chicken stock
freshly ground black pepper
2 tablespoons chopped fresh parsley
Topping:
1¼ cups whole wheat flour
1½ teaspoons baking soda
pinch salt
¾ cup oat flakes
3 tablespoons soft margarine
1 large egg
4 tablespoons plain unsweetened yogurt
½ cup Edam cheese, gratcd

Preparation time: 45 minutes
Cooking time: 1¼ hours
Oven: 350°F; then: 400°F

1. Cook the carrots and cauliflower in boiling, salted water for 5 minutes. Drain and place in a casserole.
2. Melt half the margarine and fry the leeks and fennel over moderate heat for 4 minutes, stirring frequently. Transfer to the casserole.
3. Melt the remaining margarine, stir in the flour and cook for 1 minute. Remove the pan from the heat and gradually stir in the stock. Season with salt and pepper and bring to the boil. Simmer for 3 minutes. Stir in the parsley and pour the sauce over the vegetables.
4. Cover the casserole and place in a preheated oven for 45 minutes.
5. Sift the flour, soda and salt together and tip the bran from the sieve back into the bowl. Add half the oat flakes and mix in the margarine. Beat in the egg and yogurt to make a firm dough. Shape the dough into a ball and knead lightly until it is smooth.
6. Roll out the dough on a lightly-floured board to ½ inch thick and cut into rounds with a cookie cutter.
7. Arrange the rounds on the vegetables, sprinkle with the cheese mixed with the remaining oat flakes. Increase the oven temperature and bake for 15 minutes, or until the topping is golden. Garnish with fennel fronds. Serve at once.

PISSALADIÈRE

Serves 6

1½ cups whole wheat flour
pinch salt
½ cup soft margarine
1 egg yolk
1 tablespoon plain unsweetened yogurt
1 egg white, lightly beaten
Filling:
2 tablespoons soft margarine
1 large onion, peeled and finely chopped
2 garlic cloves, peeled and crushed
1 green pepper, cored, seeded and chopped
1 teaspoon mixed dried herbs
freshly ground black pepper
1 lb tomatoes, skinned and sliced
¾ cup Gruyère cheese, grated
1½ oz can anchovy, drained
black olives, to garnish

Preparation time: 25 minutes, plus 30 minutes chilling
Cooking time: 50 minutes
Oven: 400°F; then: 350°F

1. Mix the flour and salt together and mix in the margarine, egg yolk and yogurt to form a dough – this method is particularly suitable for a food processor. Lightly knead the dough, wrap in clingfilm or foil and chill in the refrigerator until needed.
2. Melt the margarine and fry the onion, garlic and green pepper over low heat for 10 minutes, stirring frequently. Increase the heat to moderate and fry for a further 2 minutes. Stir in the herbs and season with pepper. Remove from the heat and set aside to cool.
3. Roll out the pastry on a lightly-floured board and use to line 6 greased individual flan dishes or pie tins. For easier handling the dough can be rolled between the layers of clingfilm. Trim the edges and prick the bases with a fork. Line with waxed paper and fill with dried beans.
4. Place in a preheated oven and bake for 10 minutes. Remove the beans and paper, brush the cases with egg white and return them to the oven for 5 minutes to dry.
5. Spread the onion mixture in the base of each pastry case. Arrange the tomato slices on top. Sprinkle with the cheese and make a lattice with the anchovy. Garnish with olives.
6. Reduce the oven temperature and bake for 25 minutes. Serve warm.

WHOLE WHEAT PIZZA

Serves 4

1¼ cups whole wheat flour
pinch salt
1 teaspoon baking powder
freshly ground black pepper
1 teaspoon dried oregano
¼ cup soft margarine
6 tablespoons plain unsweetened yogurt
Filling:
1 lb tomatoes, skinned and sliced
1 teaspoon soft light brown sugar
1 teaspoon dried oregano
1 large onion, peeled and sliced
2 garlic cloves, peeled and crushed
2 cups small mushrooms, thinly sliced
1 small green pepper, cored, seeded and thinly sliced into rings
1 small red pepper, cored, seeded and thinly sliced into rings
1½ cups Edam cheese, grated
10 black olives, pitted

Preparation time: 20 minutes
Cooking time: 45 minutes
Oven: 400°F

1. Mix together the flour, salt, pepper and oregano and mix in the margarine and yogurt. Form the mixture into a ball and knead it lightly until smooth. Roll out the dough on a lightly-floured board and use it to line a 10 inch greased pie pan. Line with waxed paper and fill with dried beans.
2. Place in a preheated oven and bake for 15 minutes. Remove beans and paper and return flan to oven for a further 5 minutes.
3. Put the tomatoes, sugar, oregano, onion and garlic into a pan, season with salt and pepper, stir well and bring to the boil. Simmer uncovered for 20 minutes, stirring once, until the mixture is like a thick sauce. Taste and adjust the seasoning.
4. Spread the tomato mixture over the base of the pizza. Arrange the mushrooms in a single layer and then arrange the pepper rings. Sprinkle the cheese over and garnish with the black olives.
5. Return to the oven and bake for a further 15-20 minutes, or until the cheese is brown and bubbling. Serve hot.

From the top: Pissaladière; Whole wheat pizza.

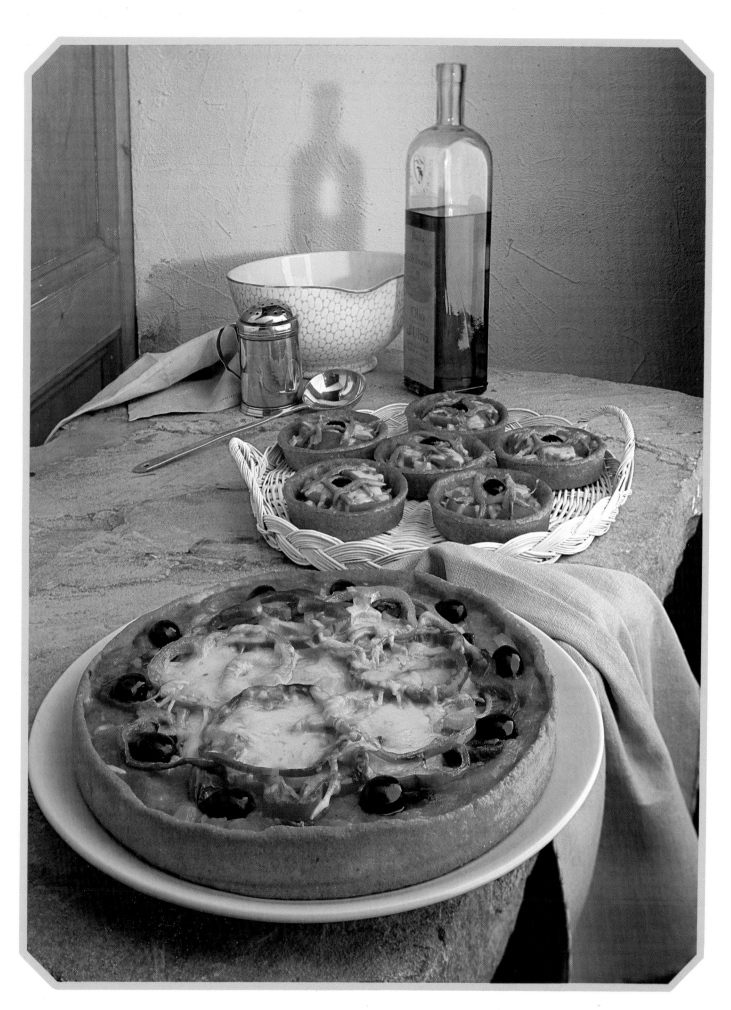

ONION TART

Serves 4-6

2 tablespoons soft margarine
2 tablespoons sunflower oil
3 onions, about 1½ lb, peeled and sliced
3 teaspoons chopped fresh thyme, or 1 teaspoon
dried thyme
1 teaspoon caraway seeds
2 eggs
¾ cup plain unsweetened yogurt
2 tablespoons heavy cream
freshly ground black pepper
Pastry:
1½ cups whole wheat flour
pinch salt
8 tablespoons vegetable shortening or margarine
1 egg yolk
about 4 tablespoons water

Preparation time: 30 minutes, plus 30 minutes chilling
Cooking time: 1 hour
Oven: 400°F; then: 350°F

1. Melt the margarine with the oil and fry the onions over moderately low heat for 20 minutes, stirring frequently, or until they are golden brown. Stir in the thyme and caraway seeds and set aside to cool.

2. For the pastry, sift the flour and salt together and tip the bran from the sieve back into the bowl. Rub in the fat until the mixture is like breadcrumbs. Stir in the egg yolk and enough water to make a firm dough. Form the dough into a ball and knead it lightly until smooth. Wrap in clingfilm or foil and chill in the refrigerator until needed.

3. Roll out the dough on a lightly-floured board and use to line a greased 8 inch pie pan. (For easier handling the dough may be rolled between two layers of clingfilm.) Trim the edges and prick the base. Line with waxed paper and fill with dried beans.

4. Place in a preheated oven and bake for 10 minutes. Remove the beans and paper and bake the case for a further 5 minutes to dry the pastry. Reduce the oven temperature.

5. Beat the eggs, yogurt and cream together and season with salt and pepper.

6. Spread the onions over the pastry case and pour on the egg mixture.

7. Bake in the oven for 30 minutes, or until the filling has set. Serve warm.

BOREKS

Serves 4

½ lb potatoes, peeled
2 medium carrots, scraped
4 tablespoons frozen peas
salt
2 tablespoons soft margarine
1 small onion, peeled and finely chopped
1 teaspoon whole wheat flour
2 teaspoons ground cumin
½ teaspoon ground ginger
pinch of chili powder
2 tablespoons chicken stock
1 large tomato, skinned and chopped
freshly ground black pepper
½ lb filo leaves
about 4 tablespoons sunflower oil

Preparation time: 1 hour
Cooking time: 40 minutes
Oven: 375°F

1. Boil the potatoes, carrots and peas until just tender. Drain. Dice the potatoes and carrots.
2. Melt the margarine and fry the onion over low heat until it is soft. Stir in the flour, cumin, ginger and chili and pour in the stock. Add the tomato and stir until it forms a paste. Season and stir in the vegetables. Set aside to cool.
3. Unroll the pastry sheets, cut into 9 × 4 inch pieces and divide into four piles.
4. Work with a quarter of the pastry at a time and cover the rest with a damp cloth to prevent drying out. Brush the pastry sheets with oil and place each one on top of the other. With the short side of the pastry facing you, place 1 heaped tablespoon of filling 2 inches from the bottom edge. Fold the left corner over the mixture. Continue folding until you have a pastry triangle enclosing the mixture with a ½ inch flap to tuck underneath. Repeat with the remaining pastry and filling.
5. Place the boreks on a greased cookie sheet. Place in a preheated oven and bake for 25 minutes or until deep golden brown and crisp.

STIR-FRIED QUARTET

Serves 4

1 small head young celery
8 oz broccoli spears
salt
4 scallions
1 red pepper, cored and seeded
2 tablespoons sunflower oil
2 inch piece fresh root ginger, peeled and cut into very thin strips
4 tablespoons blanched halved almonds
celery leaves, to garnish
Sauce:
3 tablespoons dry sherry
1 tablespoon soy sauce
1 teaspoon caster sugar
1 tablespoon light honey
¾ teaspoon ground ginger
1 tablespoon tomato paste
1 tablespoon cornstarch

Preparation time: 20 minutes
Cooking time: 15 minutes

1. Cut the vegetables into pieces of equal size and shape. Trim the celery, cut off the root end and pull off the stringy outer sticks. Thinly slice the 'heart' diagonally into ½ inch slices. Reserve some of the leaves for garnish. (Use the discarded celery for soup.)
2. Slice the broccoli stems diagonally into 1 inch pieces but leave the florets whole and blanch them in boiling, salted water for 2 minutes. Drain.
3. Slice the scallions diagonally into 2 inch pieces.
4. Core the pepper and cut into thin slices.
5. Mix the sauce ingredients together to make a thin, smooth paste.
6. Heat the oil in a thick, heavy-based skillet or wok. Stir-fry the celery and ginger over moderately high heat for 3-4 minutes, or until the celery becomes translucent. Add the broccoli, scallions and pepper and stir-fry them for 3 minutes.
7. Stir in the sauce and quickly bring to the boil, stirring. Stir-fry for 2 minutes, then add the almonds. Garnish with the celery leaves and serve at once.

Clockwise from the left: Onion tart; Boreks; Stir-fried quartet.

VEGETABLE KEBABS WITH CORIANDER RICE

Serves 4

2 medium zucchini
4 pearl onions or shallots, peeled
salt
8 small mushrooms, trimmed
4 medium tomatoes, halved, or 8 cherry tomatoes
1 red pepper, cored, seeded and cut into
2 inch squares
12 small bay leaves
Marinade:
5 tablespoons sunflower oil
1¼ tablespoons red wine vinegar
1¼ tablespoons lemon juice
1 garlic clove, peeled and crushed
2½ tablespoons chopped fresh mint
freshly ground black pepper
1 teaspoon mustard powder
Rice:
1 cup brown rice
2½ cups chicken stock
salt
1¼ teaspoons ground coriander
2½ tablespoons chopped coriander leaves
or parsley

Preparation time: 25 minutes, plus 2 hours marinating
Cooking time: 45 minutes

1. Blanch the zucchini and onions in boiling, salted water for 2 minutes. Drain.
2. Trim the zucchini and cut them into 1½ inch slices.
3. Thread all the vegetables and the bay leaves on to 4 greased skewers and lay them in a shallow dish.
4. Mix together all the marinade ingredients and pour over the kebabs. Turn in the sauce to coat the vegetables thoroughly. Cover and set aside at room temperature for about 2 hours.
5. Put the rice in a pan with the stock, salt and ground coriander. Bring to the boil, stir well, cover and simmer for 45 minutes.
6. Drain the kebabs from the sauce. Place under a preheated moderate broiler and cook for 8 minutes, turning frequently and brushing with the remaining marinade.
7. Stir the chopped coriander into the rice and spoon into a heated serving dish. Arrange the kebabs on top and serve at once. Serve with a green salad.

MIXED VEGETABLE CURRY

Serves 4

1 small cauliflower, cut into flowerets
8 oz carrots, scraped and sliced
8 oz snap beans, ends snipped, sliced
8 oz shelled fava beans
6 oz frozen corn
1 large onion, peeled and thinly sliced into rings
salt
½ cup unsalted peanuts
1 oz flaked coconut
Sauce:
2 tablespoons soft margarine
¼ cup whole wheat flour
2½ teaspoons curry powder
1¼ teaspoons ground turmeric
1¼ teaspoons ground cumin
1¼ cups milk
freshly ground black pepper
2½ tablespoons heavy cream

Preparation time: 25 minutes
Cooking time: 25 minutes

1. Steam or boil the cauliflower, carrots, beans corn and onion in salted water until they are just tender. Drain and plunge into cold water to prevent further cooking. Drain again.
2. For the sauce, melt the margarine and stir in the flour. Cook for 1 minute, then stir in the spices and cook for a further 3 minutes. Gradually stir in the milk, and bring to the boil. Simmer the sauce for 3 minutes. Season with salt and pepper and stir in the cream.
3. Stir the vegetables and peanuts into the sauce and reheat gently.
4. Turn the mixture into a heated serving dish and sprinkle with the coconut. Serve hot.

From the top: Vegetable kebabs with coriander rice; Mixed vegetable curry.

ALL THE GREENS

Serves 4

1 small ruffled endive, leaves separated
1 head Belgian endive, leaves torn in half
1 bunch watercress
½ small cucumber, thinly sliced
Dressing:
3 tablespoons olive oil
2 teaspoons red wine vinegar
¾ cup Roquefort cheese, crumbled
freshly ground black pepper
1 tablespoon plain unsweetened yogurt

Preparation time: 15 minutes

Serve as an accompaniment to a main dish or as a light meal with eggs and crispy rolls.

1. Toss together all the salad ingredients and put them into a bowl.
2. Mix the dressing.
3. Pour the dressing over the salad just before serving. Toss well.

Below, from the left: All the greens; Delicatessen delight. Opposite, from the left: Grilled pepper salad; Fennel salad.

DELICATESSEN DELIGHT

Serves 4

8 oz zucchini, thinly sliced diagonally
1 cup small mushrooms, thinly sliced
1 small onion, or shallot, peeled and thinly sliced into rings
1 head Belgian endive, leaves separated
4 oz smoked salmon, cut into matchstick strips
1 lemon, quartered, to serve
Dressing:
3 tablespoons olive oil
1 teaspoon lemon rind
1 tablespoon lemon juice
freshly ground black pepper
a pinch of cayenne pepper
1 tablespoon finely snipped chives

Preparation time: 30 minutes, plus 30 minutes marinating

1. Mix the dressing.
2. Toss together the zucchini, mushrooms and onion or shallot. Add the dressing and toss. Leave at room temperature for about 30 minutes.
3. Line a serving dish with the Belgian endive. Spoon the zucchini and mushroom salad on top and arrange the smoked salmon strips in the center. Serve with the lemon wedges.

GRILLED PEPPER SALAD

Serves 4

2 green peppers
1 red pepper
1 yellow pepper (or an extra red pepper)
2 garlic cloves, peeled and finely chopped
2 small onions, peeled and thinly sliced into rings
2 tablespoons chopped parsley
2 tablespoons black olives
1½ oz can anchovy, drained
Dressing:
3 tablespoons olive oil
2 teaspoons lemon juice
freshly ground black pepper

Preparation time: 20 minutes
Cooking time: 20 minutes

1. Place the peppers under a preheated moderately high broiler for about 15-20 minutes, turning them frequently, until their skins blacken. Cover with a damp cloth and leave them to cool. Peel.
2. Core and seed the peppers and cut them into thick slices.
3. Toss the peppers with the chopped garlic and the onion rings.
4. Bring the oil and lemon juice just to boiling point. Pour over the peppers and mix well. Leave to cool. Season with pepper.

5. Stir the parsley and olives into the salad. Turn it into a dish and garnish with the anchovy strips.

FENNEL SALAD

Serves 4-6

1 small lettuce heart, shredded
2 medium fennel bulbs, thinly sliced
2 oranges, peeled and thinly sliced into rings
1 bunch watercress
¼ cup currants
½ cup walnut halves
Dressing:
3 tablespoons sunflower oil
1 tablespoon orange juice
1 teaspoon orange rind
1 teaspoon red wine vinegar
salt
freshly ground black pepper
1 tablespoon sunflower seeds, crushed

Preparation time: 25 minutes

1. Mix the dressing.
2. Toss the lettuce and fennel together.
3. Make a ring of the orange slices around the outside of a dish. Arrange the watercress sprigs in a ring inside them.
4. Just before serving, toss the lettuce and fennel in the dressing and pile the salad in the center. Make a ring of currants around the green salad. Scatter the walnuts on top.

SPINACH VINAIGRETTE

Serves 4

1½ lb young spinach
salt
1½ tablespoons pine nuts, or blanched slivered
almonds
1 small onion, peeled and thinly sliced into rings
lemon slices, to serve
Dressing:
4 tablespoons olive oil
1 tablespoon lemon juice
2 tablespoons chopped mint
freshly ground black pepper
½ teaspoon soft light brown sugar

Preparation time: 15 minutes
Cooking time: 5 minutes

1. Wash the spinach and cook in the water clinging to the leaves in a large pan for 5 minutes or
until tender. Drain in a colander, gently pressing out the water without damaging any of the
leaves.
2. Mix all the dressing ingredients together.
3. Mix the spinach in the dressing and stir in the
pine nuts. Serve just warm or cool – but not
chilled. Garnish with the onion rings, if liked,
and serve with lemon slices.

POTATO AND PARSNIP LAYER

Serves 6

1 lb potatoes, peeled and cut into ¼ inch slices
1 large onion, peeled and thinly sliced into rings
8 oz parsnips, peeled and cut into ¼ inch slices
salt
freshly ground black pepper
pinch of grated nutmeg
1¼ cups milk or buttermilk
2 tablespoons soft margarine

Preparation time: 20 minutes
Cooking time: 2 hours
Oven: 350°F

1. Make layers of potato, onion and parsnip in a
well-greased baking dish. Dot the potatoes
with margarine and season each layer with
salt, pepper and nutmeg, finishing with a
potatoes. Pour the milk over.
2. Stand the dish on a cookie sheet and cover with
a lid or foil. Place in a preheated oven and bake
for 2 hours. Remove the covering for the last 30
minutes to brown the potatoes. Serve hot.

ARTICHOKE NESTS

Serves 4

1½ lb Jerusalem artichokes
1 tablespoon lemon juice
⅔ cup chicken stock
2 tablespoons soft margarine
4 tablespoons milk
salt
freshly ground black pepper
pinch of grated nutmeg
1 tablespoon chopped fresh mint
1 egg
¼ cup ground almonds

Preparation time: 40 minutes
Cooking time: 35 minutes
Oven: 350°F

1. Peel the artichokes and immediately drop them
into a small bowl of water, acidulated with the
lemon juice to preserve the color.
2. Cook the artichokes in the stock for 15 minutes
or until tender.
3. Drain and mash them with the margarine,
milk, salt, pepper, nutmeg and mint. Beat in
the egg and almonds. Beat to make a smooth
thick paste. Cool slightly.
4. Using a piping bag and large round nozzle,
pipe the artichoke paste on to a greased cookie
sheet to make 4 round 'nests'.
5. Place in a preheated oven and bake for 20
minutes, or until firm. Fill the nests with
cooked vegetables of your choice.

*Clockwise from the top: Spinach vinaigrette; Potato and
parsnip layer; Artichoke nests.*

VEGETABLE STRAWS

Serves 4

12 oz snap beans, ends snipped, halved if large
12 oz carrots, scraped and cut into matchstick
strips about 3½ inches long
salt
1 small red pepper, cored, seeded and sliced
into rings
1 small green pepper, cored, seeded and sliced
into rings
a few Chinese cabbage leaves, shredded
½ bunch watercress
4 tablespoons blanched almonds, toasted
Dressing:
4 tablespoons sunflower oil
1 tablespoon red wine vinegar
2 teaspoons orange juice
1 teaspoon orange rind
1 garlic clove, peeled and crushed
½ teaspoon mustard powder
1 tablespoon finely snipped chives
salt
freshly ground black pepper

Preparation time: 30 minutes
Cooking time: 10 minutes

*Serve with eggs or cheese and whole wheat bread as a light lunch
dish, or as part of a salad buffet.*

1. Cook the beans and carrots separately in boiling, salted water until they are just tender.
   Drain them, plunge them into cold water and
   drain again. Blanch the pepper rings in boiling
   salted water for 1 minute, then drain.
2. Mix the dressing.
3. Toss together the Chinese leaves, watercress
   and almonds. Pile the salad into the center of a
   flat serving dish.
4. Gather up the beans into bundles of 5 or 6 and
   push each bundle through a red pepper ring.
5. Make bundles of the carrot sticks and push
   them through a green pepper ring.
6. Arrange alternate bunches of beans and carrots around the dish. Pour the dressing over.

*Clockwise from bottom left: Vegetable straws; Italian
seafood salad; Spiced mango salad; Applemint bowl.*

ITALIAN SEAFOOD SALAD

Serves 4-6

1 lb cooked white fish fillets, such as flounder,
skinned and cut into 2 inch slices
¾ cup shelled shrimp
1½ oz can anchovy, drained and chopped
4 tablespoons black olives
2 tablespoons chopped fennel, or parsley
salad leaves, to serve
Dressing:
3 tablespoons sunflower oil
6 tablespoons dry white wine
1 tablespoon lemon juice
1 small onion or shallot, peeled and chopped
1 garlic clove, peeled and crushed
1 red pepper, cored, seeded and chopped
salt
freshly ground black pepper

Preparation time: 25 minutes
Cooking time: 5 minutes

*Serve this as a first course or, with the addition of tomato salad, it
makes a light lunch or supper dish. It also makes a good dish for
summer buffets.*

1. Put all the ingredients for the dressing into a pan and bring to the boil. Leave to cool.

2. Carefully toss together the fish, shrimp, anchovies, olives and herb. Pour on the cooled dressing and stir gently, taking care not to break up the fish.

3. Line a dish with the salad leaves. Spoon the salad on top.

APPLEMINT BOWL

Serves 4

3 apples, cored and thinly sliced
¾ cup unsalted raw peanuts
4 celery stalks, thinly sliced
mint and marjoram sprigs, to garnish
Dressing:
1 teaspoon lemon rind
2 tablespoons lemon juice
2 tablespoons chopped mint
1 tablespoon chopped marjoram, if available, or parsley
4 tablespoons plain unsweetened yogurt

Preparation time: 15 minutes

Serve with broiled meat or fish dishes. This salad is particularly suitable to accompany pork, herring and mackerel.

1. Mix the dressing until it is smooth, and have it ready before you slice the apples.

2. Toss together the apples, peanuts and celery and stir in the dressing. Toss to coat the fruit thoroughly. Garnish with the chopped mint and marjoram.

SPICED MANGO SALAD

Serves 4

1 ruffled endive, leaves separated
3 mangoes, peeled, pitted and thinly sliced
2 apples, cored and chopped
2 teaspoons lemon juice
3 tablespoons pecan nuts
Dressing:
1 egg
½ teaspoon Worcestershire sauce
1 tablespoon lemon juice
2 tablespoons plain unsweetened yogurt
salt
freshly ground black pepper

Preparation time: 20 minutes

Serve the salad with cold poultry, game or meat. It is particularly good with rich ingredients such as pork and duck.

1. Arrange the endive leaves to cover the base of a serving dish.

2. Whisk the egg together with all the other ingredients for the dressing.

3. Toss the mango in the dressing.

4. Toss the apple in the lemon juice and stir in the pecan nuts.

5. Arrange the mango slices in a wheel pattern over the endive and pour on any remaining dressing.

6. Pile the apple and nuts in the center.

GRAPEFRUIT SALAD

Serves 4-6

3 grapefruit, pink if available, peeled
and segmented
1 bunch watercress
½ small Romaine lettuce, torn into small pieces
¾ cup halved almonds, blanched and toasted
Dressing:
3 tablespoons olive oil
2 shallots, peeled and finely chopped
1 tablespoon lemon juice
1 teaspoon light honey
salt
freshly ground black pepper

Preparation time: 20 minutes

The salad is a tangy accompaniment to broiled poultry, meat and fish, and makes an interesting starter.

1. Toss together the grapefruit and watercress. Mix the dressing, pour it over the salad and toss well.
2. Line a serving dish with the lettuce leaves.
3. Just before serving, stir the almonds into the grapefruit salad and spoon it carefully on to the bed of lettuce.

DOMINO SALAD

Serves 4

1 small cauliflower, divided into florets
salt
4 oz dried garbanzos, soaked overnight and cooked
4 tablespoons black olives
1 bunch watercress
Belgian endive leaves
Dressing:
3 tablespoons olive oil
1 tablespoon cider vinegar
1 hard-cooked egg, roughly chopped
1 tablespoon sour cream
salt
freshly ground black pepper

Preparation time: 20 minutes
Cooking time: 10 minutes

1. Cook the cauliflower in boiling, salted water for about 8 minutes, until it is barely tender. Drain, plunge into cold water and drain again. Leave to cool.
2. Mix the dressing in a blender to emulsify the ingredients. Check the seasoning.
3. Mix the cauliflower, garbanzos, olives and watercress. Pour on the dressing and toss well.
4. Line a dish with the endive leaves and arrange the salad on top.

FRUIT AND NUT SALAD

Serves 4-6

8 oz shelled fava beans
salt
1 apple, cored and thinly sliced
2 pears, peeled, cored and thinly sliced
1 tablespoon water
1 tablespoon lemon juice
1 bunch watercress
2 tablespoons macadamia nuts
2 tablespoons walnut halves
1 orange, peeled and segmented
salad leaves, to serve
Dressing:
¾ cup plain unsweetened yogurt
2 tablespoons orange juice
1 tablespoon light honey
2 tablespoons chopped mint
1 scallion, thinly sliced
salt
freshly ground black pepper

Preparation time: 20 minutes, plus cooling
Cooking time: about 15 minutes

1. Mix the dressing.
2. Cook the beans in boiling, salted water until they are just tender. Drain, plunge into cold water, then drain again and cool.
3. Toss the apple and pear slices in water and lemon juice as they are cut, then drain them.
4. Mix together the beans, apple and pear slices and watercress sprigs. Pour on the dressing and toss so that the salad is well coated. Stir in the macadamia nuts.
5. Arrange in a serving dish and garnish it with the orange segments.

Clockwise from top left: Domino salad; Fruit and nut salad; Grapefruit salad.

SPROUTED BEAN SALAD

Serves 4

8 oz sprouted dried beans or peas, such as alfalfa,
or sprouted mung beans
4 scallions, thinly sliced
½ small cucumber, diced
8 large radishes, thinly sliced
5 tablespoons cashew nuts
2 hard-cooked eggs, quartered
Dressing:
⅔ cup plain unsweetened yogurt
1¼ teaspoons light honey
2½ teaspoons soy sauce
1½ teaspoons red wine vinegar
1½ tablespoons dry sherry
salt
freshly ground black pepper
Garnish:
4 scallions, cut into tassels

Preparation time: 25 minutes, plus 30 minutes soaking

*This salad can be served as a first course or as a crunchy side dish
with cold meats or fish.*

1. To make scallion tassels, remove the roots from
   the spring onions and trim to about 3 inches.
   Make 6 cuts lengthways through the stem to
   within 1½ inches of the end. Soak in iced water
   for about 30 minutes.
2. Mix the dressing and pour it into 4 individual
   serving bowls.
3. Toss together the sprouted beans, scallions,
   cucumber, radish slices and nuts. Divide the
   salad between the bowls.
4. Arrange the egg wedges on top of the salad.
   Garnish each dish with a scallion tassel.

HI-FI SALAD WITH PEANUT SAUCE

Serves 6

8 oz young snap beans, ends snipped
salt
2 leeks, thinly sliced
1 lb tomatoes, cut into wedges
4 celery stalks, sliced
1¼ tablespoons sunflower oil
1½ teaspoons lemon juice
freshly ground black pepper
1 lemon, quartered, to serve

Sauce:
1 cup unsalted peanuts
about 5 tablespoons oil
1½ tablespoons red wine vinegar
1 medium onion, peeled and chopped
1 garlic clove, peeled and halved
½-1 teaspoon chili powder (or to taste)
sugar

Preparation time: 30 minutes
Cooking time: 15 minutes

1. Cook the beans in boiling, salted water for 10 minutes, or until they are barely tender. Drain the beans, plunge them into cold water, then drain again. Toss them on crumpled paper towels and set aside to cool.
2. Grease a skillet with 1 tablespoon of the oil. Fry the peanuts for 5 minutes over moderate heat, stirring frequently. Leave the nuts to cool.
3. Grind the nuts in a blender with the remaining oil, the vinegar, onion, garlic, chili powder and sugar.
4. Toss together the beans, leeks, tomatoes and celery. Pour on the oil and lemon juice and season with pepper. Toss well.
5. Serve the salad with the lemon wedges, and the sauce separately.

Opposite: Sprouted bean salad.
Below: Hi-fi salad with peanut sauce.

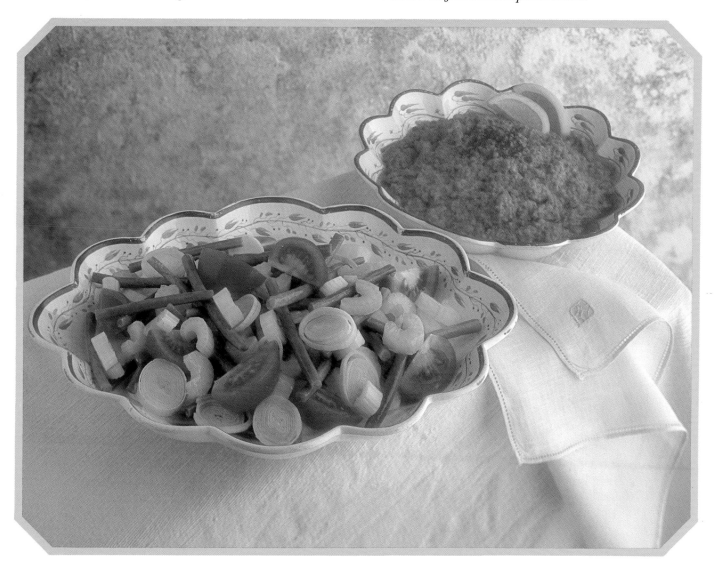

WEST INDIAN CHICKEN SALAD

Serves 6

4 celery stalks, thinly sliced
4 slices fresh pineapple, cubed
½ cup pecan nuts
2½ lb cooked chicken, skinned, boned and sliced
1 small lettuce heart, shredded
1 avocado, halved, pitted, peeled and sliced
1 tablespoon lemon juice
Dressing:
⅔ cup plain unsweetened yogurt
1 teaspoon curry powder
1 teaspoon curry paste
1 tablespoon heavy cream
1 teaspoon light honey
½ teaspoon lemon juice
salt
freshly ground black pepper

Preparation time: 35 minutes

Serve as a main course, with a tomato salad and slices of whole wheat bread.

1. Mix the dressing.
2. Toss together the celery, pineapple and pecans and pour on the dressing. Stir to mix well. Add the chicken and toss carefully to avoid breaking up the meat.
3. Arrange the lettuce in a ring around the outside of a serving dish. Toss the avocado slices in lemon juice as soon as they are cut. Arrange them over the lettuce.
4. Spoon the chicken salad into the center of the serving dish.

ROMAN SALAD

Serves 4

½ lb shelled fava beans
salt
½ lb young spinach leaves, finely shredded
1 cup mushrooms, thinly sliced
3 large firm tomatoes, skinned, seeded and chopped
a few sprigs of fennel leaves, if available, or parsley

Dressing:
3 tablespoons olive oil
1 tablespoon cider vinegar
freshly ground black pepper
1 tablespoon light honey
½ teaspoon mustard powder
50 g (2 oz) Mozzarella cheese, cubed

Preparation time: 15 minutes
Cooking time: about 15 minutes

1. Cook the beans in boiling, salted water until they are just tender. Drain, plunge at once into cold water and drain again. Leave to cool.
2. Mix the dressing.
3. Toss together the beans, spinach, mushrooms and tomatoes. Just before serving, pour on the dressing and toss well. Garnish with the fennel leaves or other herb sprigs.

SWEET CABBAGE SALAD

Serves 4

12 oz white cabbage, shredded
1 cup mushrooms, sliced
6 tablespoons golden raisins
4 tablespoons pumpkin seeds
4 tablespoons cashew nuts
Dressing:
2 tablespoons light honey
1 tablespoon lemon juice
1 teaspoon lemon rind
1 teaspoon cider vinegar
salt
pepper
3 tablespoons plain unsweetened yogurt
scallions, to garnish

Preparation time: 20 minutes, plus 30 minutes marinating

Serve as part of a cold buffet or to accompany broiled or cold poultry and meats.

1. Mix the dressing.
2. Toss together the cabbage, mushrooms and golden raisins. Pour on the dressing, toss well and leave at room temperature for about 30 minutes.
3. Stir in the pumpkin seeds and nuts.
4. Garnish with scallions.

Clockwise from the left: Sweet cabbage salad; Roman salad; West Indian chicken salad.

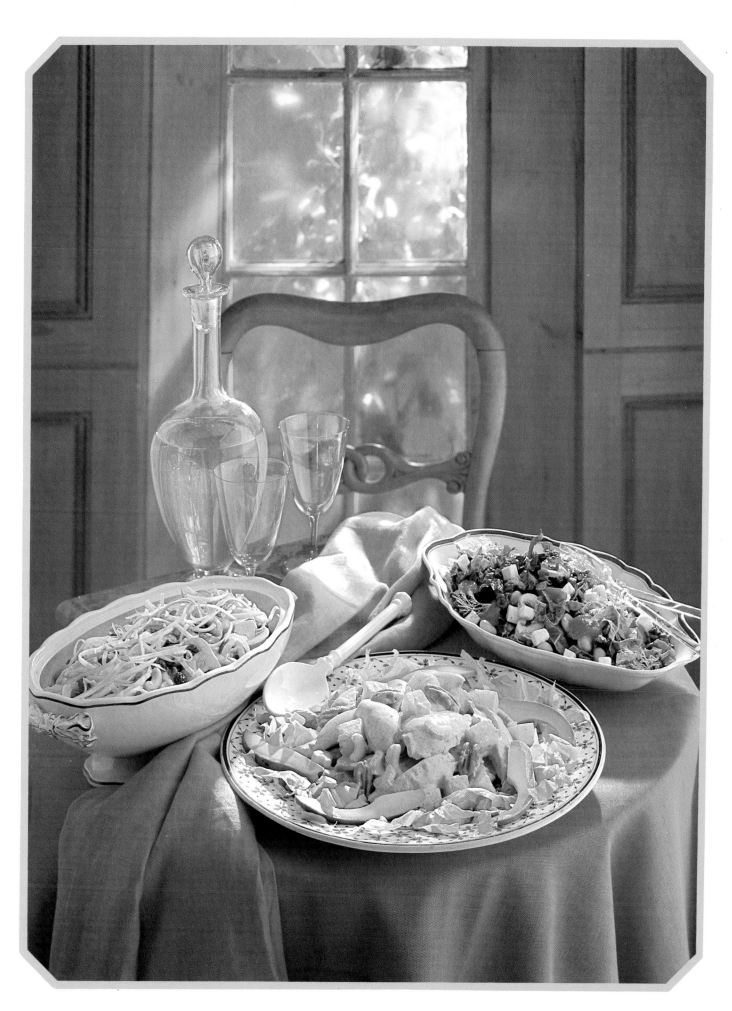

GREEK ISLAND SALAD

Serves 4-6

1 small Romaine lettuce, thinly sliced
½ small cucumber, thinly sliced
2 green peppers, cored, seeded and thinly sliced
1 large onion, peeled and thinly sliced into rings
3 large tomatoes, thinly sliced into rings
¼ lb Feta cheese, thinly sliced
salt
freshly ground black pepper
about 5 tablespoons olive oil
2½ teaspoons chopped dill, or parsley
large sprig dill or parsley, to garnish

Preparation time: 20 minutes

Serve as an accompaniment to main fish or meat dishes.

1. Arrange the salad in layers, in a glass bowl if possible, in the order in which the ingredients are listed, seasoning each layer with a little salt.

2. Pour half the oil over the tomato layer. Arrange the cheese on top and pour on the remaining oil. Sprinkle on the herb and garnish with a separate sprig.

APPLE TREE SALAD

Serves 4-6

2 dessert apples, cored and thinly sliced
2½ teaspoons lemon juice
2 cups small mushrooms, thinly sliced
8 oz black grapes, halved and pitted
2 medium carrots, scraped and grated
2½ tablespoons roasted sesame seeds
Dressing:
2½ tablespoons olive oil
1½ tablespoons apple juice
2½ tablespoons sour cream
salt
freshly ground black pepper

Preparation time: 25 minutes

This salad is equally good served as a starter or as an accompaniment to cold main dishes.

1. Mix the dressing ingredients until they are well blended.
2. Toss the apples in the lemon juice. Reserve a few apple and mushroom slices to garnish. Mix together the remaining apple and mushroom slices, the grapes, carrots and sesame seeds.
3. Pour on the dressing and mix well. Garnish the salad with the reserved apple and mushroom slices.

HIGHLAND POTATOES

Serves 4

1 lb small potatoes
salt
2 large eggs, beaten
1 tablespoon milk
freshly ground black pepper
6½ tablespoons rolled oats
1¼ tablespoons whole wheat flour
sunflower oil, for deep frying
watercress sprigs, to garnish (optional)

Preparation time: 20 minutes
Cooking time: about 20 minutes

1. Partly cook the potatoes in boiling, salted water for 12-15 minutes. Drain and leave them for about 10 minutes to cool.
2. Beat the egg and milk together and season with salt and pepper. Roll the potatoes in the egg to coat them on all sides.
3. Mix together the oats and flour. Roll or toss the potatoes in this mixture then roll again in the egg and toss once more in the mixture until they are well covered.
4. Heat the oil for deep frying to 350-375°F or until a cube of bread browns in 30 seconds. Deep-fry the potatoes in batches for about 3-4 minutes or until golden brown. Drain on kitchen paper.
5. Serve hot. Garnish with watercress sprigs if liked.

From the left: Greek island salad; Apple tree salad; Highland potatoes.

DESSERTS

There's a new style to the desserts that constitute the final flourish to a wholefood menu. Many of them bear a marked resemblance to old favorites and are reassuringly familiar, though lower in both calories and cholesterol. All the delightful and appetizing combinations of fresh fruits – cherries, peaches, plums, apricots, raspberries, strawberries, apples, melons – are there; but the dressing is likely to be devised from unsweetened fruit juices (containing natural fruit sugars) rather than a sugar-and-water syrup. There's ice cream to tingle the palate on a hot day; but the base is likely to be fruit purée rather than custard, and blended with yogurt in place of cream. And there are steamed and baked puddings to bring a glow in winter and draw attention once again to the versatility of whole grain flours. Our Christmas pudding recipe omits the traditional animal fat – suet – and so is suitable for vegetarians. It is also ideal for everyone who wants to cut down on their cholesterol intake.

Yogurt is indispensable as a cream substitute in low-calorie wholefood cooking; the new 'thick and creamy' kinds and the strained natural yogurt now so much more readily available make the healthy subterfuge almost impossible to detect.

BLACKCURRANT SESAME CRUMBLE

Serves 4-6

½ lb cooking apples, peeled, cored and
thinly sliced
12 oz blackcurrants, stripped from stalks
2 tablespoons water
3 tablespoons soft light brown sugar
Topping:
1¼ cups whole wheat flour
6 tablespoons vegetable shortening
1 oz toasted sesame seeds
3 tablespoons pale brown granulated sugar
1 teaspoon ground cinnamon

Preparation time: 20 minutes
Cooking time: 50 minutes
Oven: 325°F

Plain yogurt or soured cream go well with this pudding.

1. Simmer the apples and blackcurrants with the water for 5 minutes. Stir in the sugar. Turn the mixture into a shallow baking dish.
2. Rub together the flour and shortening until the mixture is like fine crumbs, then stir in the sesame seeds, sugar and cinnamon.
3. Sprinkle the topping over the fruit and level the top. **F**
4. Stand the dish on a cookie sheet. Bake in a preheated oven for 40-45 minutes, or until the topping is golden brown. Serve hot or warm.

F *You can freeze the uncooked pudding for up to 2 months. Bake it from frozen, in the oven at 375°F for 45-50 minutes.*

APPLE SHERBET

Serves 4

⅔ cup dry white wine
¼ cup soft light brown sugar
a strip of thinly-pared lemon rind
2 tablespoons lemon juice
a piece of fresh root ginger, peeled
1 lb cooking apples, peeled, cored and sliced
small angelica or other herb leaves, to decorate

Preparation time: 15 minutes, plus 4-5 hours freezing
Cooking time: 15 minutes

1. Put the wine, sugar, lemon rind, lemon juice and ginger into a pan and stir over a low heat until the sugar has dissolved. Increase the heat and bring to the boil.

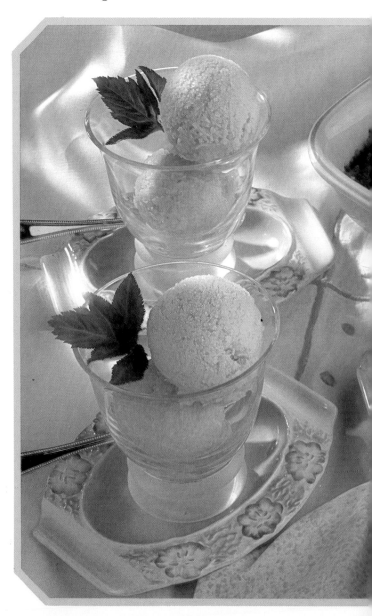

2. Add the apple slices and poach them for 8-10 minutes, or until they are tender. Remove from the heat and leave to cool.

3. Discard the lemon rind and ginger and purée the fruit and juice in a blender.

4. Pour the mixture into a container, cover with foil and freeze for 1 hour.

5. Turn the mixture into a chilled bowl and beat it to break down the ice crystals.

6. Return the mixture to the freezer for 3-4 hours, until it is firm. **F**

7. To serve, transfer the sherbet to the refrigerator for about 30 minutes. Serve it in scoops, decorated with the herb leaves.

F *You can store the sherbet for up to 2 months without loss of flavor.*

Clockwise from the left: Apple sherbet; Blackcurrant sesame crumble; Greengage brandy snap cups.

GREENGAGE BRANDY SNAP CUPS

Serves 6

½ cup whole wheat flour
½-1 teaspoon ground ginger
¼ cup soft light brown sugar
2½ tablespoons light honey
4 tablespoons soft margarine
1 teaspoon grated lemon rind
1½ teaspoons lemon juice
Filling:
1 lb greengages, pitted
2½ tablespoons water
4 tablespoons light honey
1¼ cups plain unsweetened yogurt
scented geranium leaves, to decorate
1 orange, for making the cups

Preparation time: 45 minutes
Cooking time: 40 minutes
Oven: 375°F

1. Mix together the flour and ginger. Heat the sugar, honey and margarine over a low heat and stir together until the ingredients are well blended. Remove the pan from the heat, tip in the flour and beat well. Beat in the lemon rind and lemon juice.

2. Line a cookie sheet with waxed paper. Drop teaspoonfuls of the mixture on to the cookie sheet, leaving plenty of space between them.

3. Bake in a preheated oven for 8-10 minutes. Remove the brandy snaps one at a time and – working very quickly, before they harden – press each one over an orange held in the palm of your hand to form the cups. Place the brandy snap cups upside down on a wire rack to cool. When they are completely cold, they can be stored in an airtight tin.

4. To make the filling, reserve 3 greengages to decorate and simmer the remainder in the water and honey syrup. When the greengages are soft, press them through a sieve. Return the purée to the pan and simmer until it is thick. Set aside to cool.

5. Beat together the cooled purée and the yogurt.

6. Just before serving, fill the cups with the purée. Cut the reserved greengages into thin slices and arrange a few on each cup to form a flower shape. Arrange scented geranium leaves in the center to decorate.

BROWN SUGAR MERINGUES WITH BLACKCURRANT SAUCE

Serves 4

2 egg whites
2 drops lemon juice
½ cup soft light brown sugar
1¼ teaspoons cornstarch
½ teaspoon vanilla extract
Sauce
2 cooking apples, peeled, cored and chopped
⅔ cup sweet cider
12 oz blackberries
2 tablespoons cassis syrup (optional)
Filling:
1 cup curd cheese

Preparation time: 45 minutes
Cooking time: 2¾ hours
Oven: 225°F

1. Beat the egg whites with the lemon juice until they are stiff and stand in peaks. Add half the sugar and beat until the mixture is stiff and glossy. Fold in the remaining sugar with the cornstarch and vanilla extract.

2. Line 2 cookie sheets with waxed paper. Using a pastry bag and medium star tip, pipe 8 thick S shapes and 8 swirls of meringue on to the paper.

3. Bake in the oven for 1½ hours, changing the sheets from higher to lower shelves after 45 minutes, until firm on the surface.

4. Peel the meringues from the paper and place them upside down on the trays.

5. Return the meringues to the oven for 1 hour to dry completely.

6. Cool the meringues on a wire rack. When they are cold, store them in an airtight tin.

7. Simmer the apples in the cider until they are tender. Purée them in a blender. Return to the pan and add the blackberries and cassis, if using. Simmer for 5 minutes. Serve hot or cold.

8. Just before serving, sandwich the meringues together in pairs with the cheese. Serve the sauce separately.

Below: Brown sugar meringues with blackcurrant sauce.
Opposite, from the top: Strawberry wine mousse; Frozen cranberry cheese.

1. Melt the honey in the water. Add the cranberries and simmer them for 10 minutes, or until they are tender. Leave to cool.
2. Liquidize the fruit in a blender and rub it through a sieve.
3. Beat together the cheese and sour cream. Gradually beat in the fruit purée, the syrup and orange juice. Beat until the mixture is smooth – or use a blender or food processor.
4. Turn the mixture into a decorative ¾ cup mold. Cover with foil and freeze for 4 hours.
5. To make the sauce, melt the honey in the water and orange juice. Add the cranberries and simmer for 5 minutes. Do not allow them to break up. Pour a little of the juice into the cornstarch and mix to make a smooth paste. Add the mixture to the fruit and stir gently over a low heat for 4-5 minutes until the sauce thickens and becomes transparent. Cool.
6. Unmold the dessert and leave it in the refrigerator for 1¼ hours to soften. Decorate with mint leaves. Serve the sauce separately.

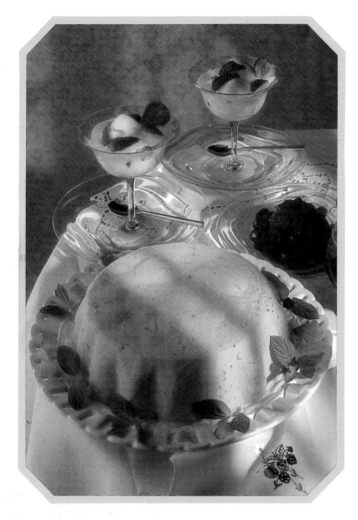

FROZEN CRANBERRY CHEESE

Serves 6

3 oz heavy honey
2 tablespoons water
6 oz fresh or frozen cranberries
1½ cups curd cheese
⅔ cup sour cream
3 tablespoons grenadine or rosehip syrup
1 tablespoon orange juice
mint leaves, to decorate
Sauce:
2 tablespoons heavy honey
2 tablespoons water
2 tablespoons orange juice
6 oz fresh or frozen cranberries
1 teaspoon cornstarch

*Preparation time: 30 minutes, plus 4 hours freezing
Cooking time: 25 minutes*

This is a lovely 'alternative Christmas pudding', to make when fresh cranberries are in season – though frozen ones are good too.

STRAWBERRY WINE MOUSSE

Serves 6

1¼ cups plain unsweetened yogurt
2 teaspoons orange rind
1 tablespoon orange juice
¼ cup soft light brown sugar
½ cup rosé wine
1 lb strawberries, halved if large

Preparation time: 20 minutes, plus 1 hour chilling

This dessert is best made shortly before serving. If it is left for more than an hour or so, the wine may separate and sink to the bottom. But it's still delicious!

1. Beat the yogurt with the orange rind and orange juice. Beat in the sugar, then gradually pour on the wine, beating all the time. Chill in the refrigerator for at least 1 hour.
2. Reserve a few of the best strawberries to decorate. Lightly stir the remainder into the mousse.
3. Pour the dessert into a bowl or 6 individual glasses and decorate with the reserved strawberries.

ICED GINGER MERINGUE

Serves 6-8

2 egg whites
3½ oz soft light brown sugar
½-1 teaspoon ground ginger
1¼ cups plain unsweetened yogurt
5 tablespoons heavy cream
2½ teaspoons grated lemon rind
2 teaspoons lemon juice
Sauce:
12 oz raspberries
2½ tablespoons lemon juice
2½ tablespoons light honey

Preparation time: 40 minutes, plus about 3 hours freezing
Cooking time: 3 hours
Oven: 225°F

1. Whisk the egg whites until they are stiff, then whisk in half the sugar until the mixture is stiff and glossy. Mix the remaining sugar with the ground ginger and fold into the egg whites.
2. Line a cookie sheet with waxed paper and spoon on mounds of the mixture.
3. Bake the meringues in a preheated oven for 2½-3 hours, until they are dry.
4. Cool the meringues on a wire rack. Peel them from the paper and leave them to become completely cold. **Ⓐ**
5. Whip together the yogurt and cream and beat in the lemon rind and lemon juice. Crush the meringues into chunks and stir them into the mixture.
6. Line a 3-cup bread pan with foil and turn the mixture into it. Cover with foil and freeze for about 3 hours. There is no need to stir the mixture again.
7. Sieve the raspberries and stir in the lemon juice and honey.
8. Unmold the meringue on to a serving platter and leave it in the refrigerator for 30 minutes before serving.
9. Pour a little of the sauce over it to decorate and serve the rest separately.

Ⓐ *You can make the brown sugar meringues well in advance and store them in an airtight tin.*

Clockwise from the left: Iced ginger meringue; Set-alight salad; Honeyed Greek yogurt.

HONEYED GREEK YOGURT

Serves 4

2½ cups plain unsweetened yogurt
2½ tablespoons sweet sherry
4 tablespoons clear honey
1¼ tablespoons soft dark brown sugar
8 fresh figs, quartered

Preparation time: 15 minutes, plus 2 hours chilling

1. Beat the yogurt, sherry and honey. Decorate with sugar, cover and chill for at least 2 hours.

2. Just before serving, cut the fresh figs into quarters and serve with the yogurt.

SET-ALIGHT SALAD

Serves 6

⅔ cup red grape juice
2 tablespoons water
1 tablespoon lemon juice
2 bay leaves
1 lb redcurrants, stripped from stalks
½ lb gooseberries, topped and tailed
½ lb raspberries
2 tablespoons brandy

Preparation time: 30 minutes
Cooking time: 10 minutes

1. Bring the grape juice, water, lemon juice and bay leaves to the boil in a large pan and simmer for 3 minutes. **A**
2. Add the redcurrants and gooseberries and bring to the boil in the syrup. Simmer for 3-4 minutes. Add the raspberries and just return to the boil. Transfer the fruit and syrup to a serving dish.
3. Pour the brandy into a warmed ladle and set light to it. Pour the flaming brandy on to the fruit. Serve at once.

A *You can prepare the syrup in advance, then quickly reheat it when you have prepared all the fruit and are ready to serve the dessert.*

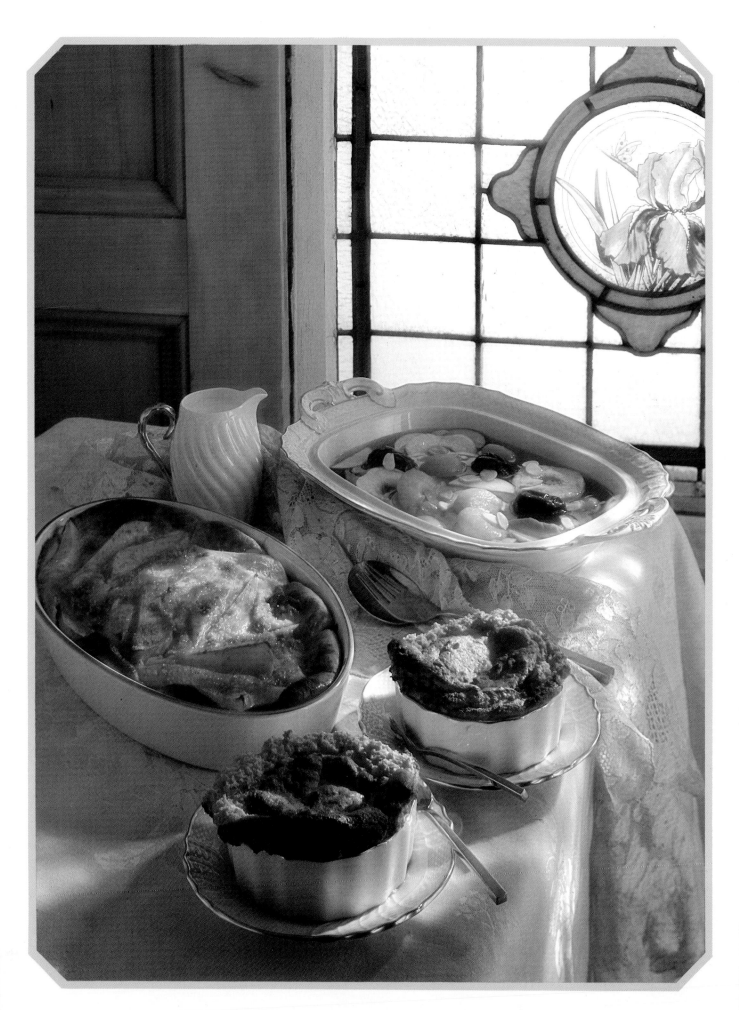

PEAR CLAFOUTI

Serves 4

⅓ cup whole wheat flour
pinch salt
½ cup soft light brown sugar
2 eggs
1 egg yolk
1 tablespoon sunflower oil
1¼ cups milk
1 lb dessert pears, peeled, cored and sliced
1 tablespoon lemon juice

Preparation time: 20 minutes
Cooking time: 45 minutes
Oven: 350°F

1. Mix together the flour, a pinch of salt and all but 2 tablespoons sugar. Beat in the eggs, the egg yolk and the oil. Gradually pour on the milk, beating constantly.
2. Toss the pears in the lemon juice and arrange them in a greased, shallow baking dish. Pour on the batter.
3. Bake the pudding in a preheated oven for 30 minutes. Dust with the remaining sugar and bake for a further 10-15 minutes. Serve hot.

GINGERED FRUITS

Serves 6

1 lb mixed dried fruits – apple rings, apricots, peaches, pears, prunes, soaked overnight in 2½ cups water
1 piece fresh root ginger, peeled and halved
4 tablespoons ginger wine
2 teaspoons lemon juice
2 dessert apples, cored and thinly sliced
2 tablespoons blanched almonds, toasted
Sauce:
1 cup plain unsweetened yogurt
2 pieces candied ginger, finely chopped
1 tablespoon ginger syrup
1 teaspoon lemon juice

Preparation time: 10 minutes, plus overnight soaking
Cooking time: 30 minutes

Clockwise from the top: Gingered fruits; Plum soufflé; Pear clafouti.

1. Put the fruits in a pan with the remaining soaking water, the pieces of ginger, ginger wine and lemon juice and bring slowly to the boil. Simmer for 25 minutes, or until the fruits are tender. Leave to cool.
2. Remove the ginger. Stir in the apple slices and, just before serving, the toasted almonds.
3. Mix together the yogurt, chopped ginger, syrup and lemon juice.
4. Serve the fruits cold but not chilled, with the sauce separately.

PLUM SOUFFLÉ

Serves 4

1 lb dessert plums, stoned
2 teaspoons lemon juice
2 tablespoons water
2 tablespoons whole wheat semolina
2 tablespoons ground almonds
2 eggs, separated
2 tablespoons Amaretto liqueur (optional)
4 tablespoons blanched flaked almonds, toasted

Preparation time: 40 minutes
Cooking time: 45 minutes
Oven: 375°F

1. Simmer the plums with the lemon juice and water until they are tender. Press them through a sieve. Return the purée to the pan and stir in the semolina. Bring to the boil and simmer for 10 minutes. Cool.
2. Beat the ground almonds into the cooled purée. Beat in the egg yolks and liqueur.
3. Whisk the egg whites until they are stiff. Fold them into the fruit mixture.
4. Spoon the mixture into 4 greased individual soufflé dishes. Stand them in a roasting pan with water to come half way up the sides.
5. Bake the soufflés in a preheated oven for 20 minutes, or until the mixture is just set.
6. Scatter the almonds on top and serve at once.

MINT ICE FOLDS

Serves 4

⅓ cup soft light brown sugar
⅔ cup water
2 oz fresh mint
2½ tablespoons lemon juice
1¼ cups plain unsweetened yogurt
Sauce:
2 medium cooking apples, peeled, cored
and chopped
2½ tablespoons water
4 tablespoons crème de menthe liqueur
2½ tablespoons light honey
1¼ tablespoons lemon juice
To garnish:
mint sprigs

Preparation time: 30 minutes, plus 4-5 hours freezing
Cooking time: 20 minutes

1. Put the sugar and water into a pan and stir over low heat to dissolve the sugar. Add the mint leaves, bring to the boil and simmer for 5 minutes. Remove from the heat and leave to become completely cold.
2. Strain off the mint leaves, pressing them against the sieve to extract all the moisture and flavor.
3. Stir the lemon juice into the cold syrup. Pour it into the yogurt, beating constantly.
4. Pour the mixture into a container, cover with foil and freeze for 1 hour.
5. Turn the partly frozen mixture into a chilled bowl and beat it thoroughly to break down the ice crystals.
6. Return the mixture to the freezer for 3-4 hours, until it is firm.
7. To make the sauce, simmer the apples in the water until they are mushy. Beat them well or liquidize them in a blender, then stir in the liqueur, honey and lemon juice. Simmer for 3-4 minutes, stirring frequently. Leave to cool.
8. Transfer the sherbet to the refrigerator for 30 minutes. Scoop it from the container with a tablespoon and arrange the "folds" on a dish. Decorate with the mint sprigs. Serve the sauce separately.

Clockwise from the left: Mint ice folds; Corinth pancakes; Red fruit salad.

RED FRUIT SALAD

Serves 4

1½ lb raspberries
5 tablespoons light honey
8 oz sweet cherries, pitted
8 oz black currants, stripped from stems
Curd cheese:
2½ teaspoons powdered gelatin
2½ tablespoons hot water
1½ cups cottage cheese, sieved
⅔ cup plain unsweetened yogurt
5 tablespoons heavy cream
freshly grated nutmeg

Preparation time: 30 minutes, plus overnight draining
Cooking time: 5 minutes

1. Sprinkle the gelatin on the water in a small bowl. Stir well and stand the bowl in hot water

to dissolve the crystals.

2. Beat together the cottage cheese, the yogurt and the cream, then stir in the dissolved gelatin.

3. Spoon the mixture into 4 draining molds or yogurt pots. To use yogurt pots, cover them with muslin and invert them to drain over a dish. Leave overnight.

4. Liquidize half the raspberries, then sieve them. Stir the honey into the purée over a low heat. Stir in the remaining raspberries, the cherries and blackcurrants and simmer for 2-3 minutes. Cool, then chill in the refrigerator for at least 1 hour. F

5. Turn out the curd cheese molds and decorate them with a pinch of grated nutmeg. Serve them with the fruit salad as a substantial 'sauce'.

F *The fruit salad can be frozen, but not the curd cheese molds.*

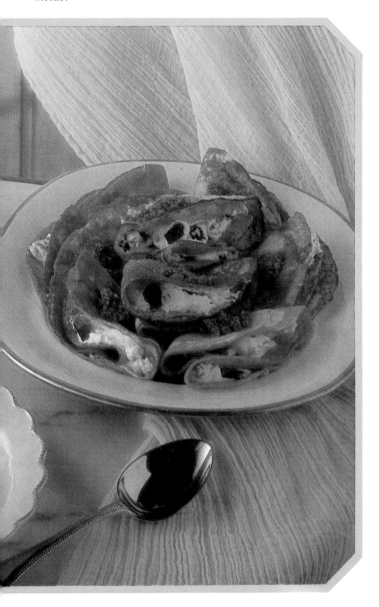

CORINTH PANCAKES

Makes 8 pancakes

1 cup whole wheat flour
salt
1 egg, beaten
¾ cup unsweetened orange juice
1 cup soda water
oil or fat, for frying
light brown sugar, for sprinkling
Filling:
1 cup curd cheese
½ cup plain unsweetened yogurt
1 tablespoon lemon rind
2 teaspoons lemon juice
¾ cup currants
⅓ cup dried pitted dates, chopped

Preparation time: 20 minutes
Cooking time: 45 minutes

1. Mix together the flour and salt and beat in the egg. Gradually beat in the orange juice and soda water.

2. Use the minimum of oil or fat to grease an 8 inch omelette pan. When the pan is hot, pour in enough of the batter to cover the base with a thin film. Cook until the pancake is brown and bubbling on the underside. Flip or toss and cook the other side.

3. Keep the cooked pancakes warm while you make the remainder of the batch.

4. Beat together the cheese, yogurt, lemon rind and lemon juice. Stir in the currants and dates.

5. Spread the mixture over each pancake. Fold each one in half, then in half again, so that they are wedge-shaped.

6. Arrange the pancakes in a heated flameproof dish. Sprinkle on the sugar and cook them under a preheated moderate broiler for 3-4 minutes until the sugar caramelizes.

CHRISTMAS PUDDING

Serves 12

1 cup soft margarine
2 eggs, beaten
1 cup whole wheat flour
2 cups fresh whole wheat breadcrumbs
1 teaspoon mixed ground spice
1 teaspoon ground cinnamon
½ teaspoon ground nutmeg
1½ cups seedless raisins
1½ cups currants
¾ cup golden raisins
1⅓ cups dried pitted dates, chopped
⅓ cup dried figs, chopped
½ cup blanched chopped almonds
½ cup hazelnuts, chopped
3 tablespoons molasses
2 tablespoons orange rind
4 tablespoons orange juice
¾ cup milk
4 tablespoons brandy

Preparation time: 1¼ hours
Cooking time: 4 hours

1. Beat the margarine and gradually beat in the eggs. In a separate bowl, mix together the flour, breadcrumbs and spices and stir them into the egg mixture. Stir in all the remaining ingredients. Beat well until all the liquid has been evenly incorporated.
2. Divide the mixture between 2 greased 1½ pint pudding basins. Cover them with a piece of waxed paper and foil, pleated along the center to allow for rising.
3. Place the basins on a trivet in 2 pans and pour in fast-boiling water to come half-way up the sides. Cover the pans and steam for 4 hours, topping up with more boiling water as needed.
4. Lift out the puddings and cool them on a wire rack. Replace the covers with fresh, greased greaseproof paper and foil. When they are completely cold, store them in a cool dry place for up to 1 year.
5. To reheat the puddings, steam them in a covered pan of fast-boiling water for 2½ hours.

Above: Christmas pudding.
Opposite, from the left: Plum brûlée; Nomad pudding.

PLUM BRÛLÉE

Serves 6

1½ lb sweet plums
2½ tablespoons soft light brown sugar
Topping:
2 cups whole milk plain unsweetened yogurt
⅔ cup sour cream
¼ cup soft light brown sugar

Preparation time: 20 minutes, plus several hours chilling
Cooking time: 10 minutes

1. Blanch the plums in boiling water for 2 minutes. Drain them.
2. Halve and pit the plums and arrange them, cut sides down, in a flameproof dish. Sprinkle on the sugar.
3. Beat together the yogurt and sour cream.
4. Spread the yogurt mixture over the fruit, cover and chill in the refrigerator for several hours, or overnight.
5. About 2 hours before serving, sprinkle the sugar evenly over the yogurt topping.
6. Place under a preheated medium hot grill and cook for 5 minutes, or until the sugar topping has caramelized. Cool, then chill.

NOMAD PUDDING

Serves 6

2½ cups milk
1½ oz whole wheat semolina
¼ cup soft light brown sugar
2 eggs, beaten
2½ teaspoons rosewater
½ cup ground almonds
rose petals, to decorate
¼ cup pistachio nuts, chopped, to decorate

Preparation time: 10 minutes
Cooking time: 30 minutes

1. Put the milk in a pan and sprinkle on the semolina, stirring constantly. Add the sugar and bring to the boil, still stirring.
2. Simmer for 15 minutes, until the mixture has thickened.
3. Remove the pan from the heat, cool slightly and beat in the eggs, rosewater and almonds. Return to the heat and simmer very gently for 10 minutes.
4. Pour the mixture into 6 small greased individual dishes. Leave them to cool.
5. Decorate the puddings with the rose leaves and sprinkle with chopped nuts. Serve cold but not chilled.

BAKING

Wholefood baking really means turning back the clock – shades of huge farm kitchens, roaring fires, a griddle iron over the ashes – and appreciating once again good wholesome *whole* ingredients. It means using whole grain flours, milled complete with the cereal germ and bran and consequently still retaining the nutrients and the natural dietary fibre which are processed out of refined white products.

Black raisin loaf, Honey spice ring, Fennel rye bread, Walnut spongecake gâteau – all have a characteristic homeliness and a delicious nutty texture that more than compensates for the fact that, baked with the whole grain, they will never be light as a feather.

Bread, baking powder biscuits and quickbreads, lowest in fat and sugar content, make sound nutritional sense for everyday baking. As our recipes show, you can ring the changes with herbs, spices and fruits (and increase the proportion of dried fruits to cut down still further on the sugar) until you and the family are spoiled for choice. Cutting down on sugars is essential to the spirit of wholefood cookery and it need be absolutely no hardship as you will find when you try our sugarless Celebration cake.

FENNEL RYE BREAD

Makes one 1 lb loaf

1½ cups whole wheat flour
1½ cups rye flour
1 teaspoon salt
2 teaspoons baking powder
4 tablespoons soft margarine
¾ cup sour cream
1 egg
milk, for brushing
1 tablespoon fennel seeds

Preparation time: 25 minutes
Cooking time: 1¼ hours
Oven: 400°F

1. Sift together the flours, salt and baking powder and tip in any bran remaining in the sieve. Rub in the margarine. Beat together the sour cream and egg and stir into the dry ingredients to form a firm dough.
2. Knead the dough on a lightly-floured board until it is smooth. Shape it into a round and place it on a greased cookie sheet. Brush the top of the loaf with milk and sprinkle on the fennel seeds.
3. Bake in a preheated oven for 1¼ hours, or until the bread sounds hollow when tapped. Transfer it to a wire rack to cool. ☐F The bread is best eaten within 1 day of baking.

☐F *Freeze for up to 1 month. Thaw the baked loaf at room temperature for 6-7 hours.*

SESAME BAGELS

Makes 16 rings

3 cups whole wheat flour
5 tablespoons sesame seeds
1 teaspoon salt
1 teaspoon soft light brown sugar
2 tablespoons fast-acting dried yeast
⅔ cup milk
9 tablespoons hot water
2 tablespoons sunflower oil
1 egg, beaten

Preparation time: ½ hour, plus 2 hours rising
Cooking time: 35 minutes
Oven: 425°F

Serve Sesame Bagels hot, as a snack, or to accompany a light meal of soup or salad.

1. Mix the flour, 3 tablespoons of the sesame seeds, the salt, sugar and yeast. Mix together the milk, water, oil and egg, and pour on to the dry ingredients. Beat to form a firm dough in a food processor or knead for at least 10 minutes by hand.

2. Cut the dough into 16 pieces and roll them into balls. Use the oiled handle of a wooden spoon to push a hole through the center of each one.

3. Place the rings on a greased cookie sheet. Leave in a warm place to rise for about 1¾ hours loosely covered with a clean cloth.

4. Bring a large pan of water to the boil and poach the bagels in batches for 30-45 seconds, until they expand. Lift them out with a draining spoon and dry them on crumpled pieces of kitchen paper.

5. Bake the bagels in a preheated oven for 25-30 minutes, until they are well risen. Brush lightly with sunflower oil and toss at once in the remaining sesame seeds. Serve hot.

WHEAT GERM BREAD

Makes two loaves

3½ cups strong whole wheat flour
1 cup bran
¾ cup wheatgerm
1 tablespoon soft light brown sugar
2 tablespoons fast-acting dried yeast
2 teaspoons salt
1½ cups tepid water
2 tablespoons sunflower oil
2 tablespoons caraway seeds, for topping

Preparation time: 25 minutes, plus 1 ½ hours rising
Cooking time: 35 minutes
Oven: 450°F; then: 400°F

1. Grease two 3-cup bread pans.
2. Mix together the flour, bran, wheatgerm, sugar, yeast and salt. Pour on the water and oil and mix to a firm dough.
3. Process the dough or knead on a lightly-floured board for 10 minutes, or until it is smooth.
4. Divide the dough into pieces of equal size.
5. Press the dough into the prepared pans and level the tops. Brush with water and sprinkle on the caraway seed topping.
6. Cover the pans and leave them in a warm place to rise for 1½ hours, until the dough is risen. This mixture will only rise part way up the pans.
7. Bake the loaves in a preheated oven for 5 minutes. Reduce the heat and bake for 30 minutes more. The loaves should sound hollow when tapped.
8. Stand the loaves in their pans on a wire rack to cool. ℉

℉ *Thaw the loaves at room temperature for 5-6 hours.*

From the left: Wheat germ bread; Walnut spongecake gâteau.

WALNUT SPONGECAKE GÂTEAU

Makes one 7½ inch cake

1⅓ cups whole wheat flour
2½ teaspoons baking powder
¾ cup soft margarine
1¼ cups soft light brown sugar
¾ cup walnuts, finely chopped
2 teaspoons grated lemon rind
3 eggs
1 tablespoon lemon juice
Filling and topping:
1½ cups curd cheese
about 3 tablespoons light honey
3 peaches, pitted, skinned and thinly sliced
1 tablespoon lemon juice

Preparation time: 30 minutes
Cooking time: 40 minutes
Oven: 350°F

1. Grease two 7½ inch cake pans.
2. Sift the flour and baking powder, reserving the bran. Add the margarine, sugar, walnuts, lemon rind and eggs and beat well until the mixture is smooth. Beat in the lemon juice.
3. Divide the mixture between the cake pans. Level the tops, then make a very slight dip in the center of each. Sprinkle over bran.
4. Bake in a preheated oven for 35-40 minutes, until the cakes are firm but springy to the touch.
5. Stand the pans on a wire rack to cool. Turn out the cakes and leave them to become completely cold. **F**
6. Beat the cheese and honey and add a little more honey if the mixture still tastes salty. Toss the peach slices in the lemon juice as soon as they are cut.
7. Spread half the cheese on to one half of the cake as a filling, and arrange most of the peach slices on top. Spread the remaining cheese on top of the second layer. Sandwich the 2 layers together and decorate the top with the reserved peach slices.

F *Freeze the 2 sponge sandwich layers separately, close-wrapped in foil. Thaw at room temperature for 4 hours.*

APRICOT CAKE

Makes one 7 inch cake

½ cup soft margarine
¾ cup soft light brown sugar
2 large eggs, beaten
1½ cups whole wheat flour
2½ teaspoons baking powder
½ teaspoon ground cinnamon
1½ cups dried apricots, soaked, drained
and chopped
¾ cup seedless raisins
2 tablespoons light brown sugar
5 tablespoons unsweetened orange juice
Topping:
¾ cup dried apricots, soaked and drained
¾ cup sour cream
1 tablespoon light honey
2 tablespoons blanched almonds, toasted
and chopped

Preparation time: 35 minutes
Cooking time: 1½ hours
Oven: 325°F

1. Grease and line a 7 inch cake pan.
2. Beat the margarine and sugar together until it is light and fluffy, then gradually beat in the eggs. Sift the flour, baking powder and cinnamon and tip in any bran left in the sieve. Add the dry ingredients, a little at a time to the creamed mixture. Stir in the apricots and raisins and beat well.
3. Turn the mixture into the prepared cake pan, level the top and sprinkle on the sugar.
4. Bake in a pre-heated oven for 1¼-1½ hours, or until a skewer pierced through the center of the cake comes out clean.
5. Stand the cake in its pan on a wire rack to cool. Then peel off the paper and leave the cake to become completely cool. F
6. Liquidize the apricots in a blender and beat in the sour cream and honey.
7. Spread the topping over the cake. Sprinkle the chopped nuts around the edge, to decorate.

F *Open-freeze the cake, then close-wrap it in foil and freeze for up to 6 months. Thaw at room temperature for 6-7 hours.*

CAROB HONEY CAKE

Makes one 8 inch flat cake

⅔ cup soft light brown sugar
½ cup light honey
½ cup whole wheat flour
3 tablespoons carob powder
½ teaspoon ground cinnamon
⅓ cup ground almonds
1 tablespoon grated orange rind
⅓ cup candied orange peel, chopped
1¼ cups hazelnuts
¾ cup blanched almonds, lightly toasted

Preparation time: 20 minutes
Cooking time: 45 minutes
Oven: 275°F

To store the cake, close-wrap it in foil once it is cold and put it in a container in the refrigerator. If the cake is left for very long at room temperature it soon becomes sticky.

1. Melt the sugar and honey over a low heat, then bring to simmering point and simmer, stirring frequently, for 10 minutes.
2. Sift the flour, carob powder and cinnamon, tip in any bran left in the sieve and stir in the ground almonds and orange rind. Pour on the honey mixture, and stir in the peel and nuts. Beat thoroughly, working quickly as the mixture sets.
3. Spread the mixture into an 8 inch greased and floured loose-based cake pan.
4. Bake in a preheated oven for 30-45 minutes, until the cake is firm.
5. Cool the cake in the flan ring on a wire rack.

SPICY CARROT CAKE

Makes one 9 inch cake

2 medium bananas, mashed
1 cup soft light brown sugar
3 eggs, beaten
2 cups whole wheat flour
1 teaspoon baking soda
1 teaspoon salt
2 teaspoons baking powder
1 teaspoon mixed ground spice
½ cup walnuts, chopped
¾ cup sunflower oil
1¾ cups carrot, grated
Topping:
¾ cup low fat soft cheese
⅓ cup soft light brown sugar
1 teaspoon lemon rind
2 teaspoons lemon juice
lemon slices, quartered to decorate

Preparation time: 30 minutes
Cooking time: 1-1¼ minutes
Oven: 350°F

1. Grease and line a 9 inch round cake pan.
2. Beat the bananas and sugar until they are well blended. Gradually beat in the eggs. Sift the flour, soda, salt, baking powder and spice, reserving the bran, and beat into the banana mixture a little at a time with the chopped walnuts. Beat in the oil, then stir in the grated carrot. Beat well until the mixture is smooth.
3. Turn the mixture into the prepared cake pan. Level the top and sprinkle on the reserved bran.
4. Bake in a preheated oven for about 1-1¼ hours, or until the cake is 'set' and golden brown. Test by piercing it through the center with a fine skewer, which should come out clean if the cake is done.
5. Leave the cake in the tin and place on a wire rack to cool. Then peel off the paper and leave the cake to become completely cold.
6. Mix together in a bowl the cheese, sugar, lemon rind and juice.
7. Spread the mixture over the top of the cake. Arrange the lemon slices on top to decorate.

Clockwise from the top: Carrot cake; Carob honey cake; Apricot cake.

CELEBRATION CAKE

Makes one 8 inch cake

1⅓ cups dried pitted dates, finely chopped
¾ cup milk, plus extra if needed (see method)
½ cup soft margarine
3 eggs, beaten
1½ cups whole wheat flour
2 teaspoons baking powder
1 teaspoon ground cinnamon
½ teaspoon ground ginger
a large pinch of grated nutmeg
2 teaspoons grated orange rind
3 tablespoons orange juice
⅔ cup ground almonds
½ cup blanched almonds, chopped
1½ cups seedless raisins
1 cup currants
½ cup golden raisins
⅓ cup candied orange peel, chopped
Apricot paste:
4 oz blanched almonds
1½ cups dried apricots, chopped
2 tablespoons soft light brown sugar
1 tablespoon lemon juice
1 tablespoon light honey, warmed

Preparation time: 1 hour
Cooking time: 2-2½ hours
Oven: 300°F

1. Grease an 8 inch cake pan and line it with waxed paper.
2. Mash the dates with the milk and heat them over a very low heat, stirring constantly, until they form a thick paste. Set aside to cool.
3. Beat the cooled date paste with the margarine. Beat in the eggs, a little at a time.
4. Sift the flour, baking powder and spices. Add any bran left in the sieve and the orange rind.
5. Gradually add the dry ingredients to the date mixture, beating all the time. Beat in the orange juice, ground and chopped almonds, raisins, currants, golden raisins and peel. Beat the mixture well and add a little milk if necessary to give a firm dropping consistency.
6. Turn the mixture into the prepared pan and level the top.
7. Bake in a preheated oven for 2-2½ hours, until a fine skewer pierced through the center of the cake comes out clean.
8. Leave the cake in the pan and stand it on a wire rack to cool. **F**

9. To make the apricot paste, grind the almonds until they are as fine as semolina. Reserve 2 teaspoons of the ground almonds, then add the apricots, sugar and lemon juice and process to a smooth paste. Knead the paste on a board lightly sprinkled with the remaining ground almonds. **A**
10. Roll out the paste to a thickness of ¼ inch and cut out decorative shapes, and a thick band to cover the side of the cake. Brush the sides of the

cake with the honey and press on the strip of apricot paste. Ⓐ Ⓕ Brush the decoration for the top with honey and press on to the top of the cake. Close-wrap the cake in foil and store it in an airtight tin.

Ⓐ *You can make the apricot paste in advance, wrap it in foil and store it in an airtight container. You can also store the cut-out shapes, stacked between layers of greaseproof paper or polythene.*
Ⓕ *Prewrap the cake when cold and freeze for up to 3 months. Thaw at room temperature.*

HONEY SPICE RING

Makes 1¾ pint ring cake

⅔ cup soft margarine
½ cup soft light brown sugar
3 tablespoons light honey
2 eggs, beaten
1⅓ cups whole wheat flour
½ teaspoon baking powder
1½ teaspoons mixed ground spice
½ teaspoon ground ginger
¾ cup walnuts, chopped
Filling:
¾ cup cottage cheese, sieved
⅔ cup plain unsweetened yogurt
½ cup soft light brown sugar
⅓ cup candied orange peel, chopped
½ cup seedless raisins
¼ cup blanched almonds, chopped
1 tablespoon orange rind

Preparation time: overnight draining, then 1 hour
Cooking time: 35-40 minutes
Oven: 350°F

1. Grease and flour a 4½ cup tube pan.
2. Prepare the filling the day before. Beat the cheese, yogurt and sugar. Stir in the peel, raisins, almonds and orange rind and beat well.
3. Line a sieve with a double layer of scalded muslin. Spoon in the cheese filling, cover it with muslin and put a plate and heavy weight on top. Leave the cheese to drain for about eight hours or overnight.
4. Cream the margarine, sugar and honey until the mixture is light and fluffy. Stir in the eggs. Sift the flour, baking powder and spices. Fold the flour into the creamed mixture and stir in the walnuts.
5. Spoon the mixture into the prepared pan and sprinkle the top with the reserved bran.
6. Stand the mold on a cookie sheet and bake in a preheated oven for 35-40 minutes, until the cake is well risen.
7. Leave the cake to cool in the mold, then turn it out on to a wire rack until completely cold.
8. Turn the cake on to a serving dish. Fork over the cheese filling and spoon some into the center of the ring.

Variation: *The cheese filling is a simple adaptation of the Russian Easter dessert known as pashka. It is also delicious served with fresh or simmered soft fruits.*

From the top: Celebration cake; Honey spice ring (variation).

ACKNOWLEDGEMENTS

The publishers would like to thank the following
who were involved in the preparation of this book:
Photographer James Jackson with stylist Sue
Russell
Food prepared for photography by Allyson Birch
Illustrations by Jane Brewster